THE STRATEGIC IMPORTANCE OF THE WESTERN HEMISPHERE: DEFINING U.S. INTERESTS IN THE REGION

HEARING

BEFORE THE

SUBCOMMITTEE ON THE WESTERN HEMISPHERE

OF THE

COMMITTEE ON FOREIGN AFFAIRS HOUSE OF REPRESENTATIVES

ONE HUNDRED FOURTEENTH CONGRESS

FIRST SESSION

FEBRUARY 3, 2015

Serial No. 114–12

Printed for the use of the Committee on Foreign Affairs

Available via the World Wide Web: http://www.foreignaffairs.house.gov/ or http://www.gpo.gov/fdsys/

U.S. GOVERNMENT PUBLISHING OFFICE

93–156PDF   WASHINGTON : 2015

For sale by the Superintendent of Documents, U.S Government Publishing Office
Internet: bookstore.gpo.gov   Phone: toll free (866) 512–1800; DC area (202) 512–1800
Fax: (202) 512–2104   Mail: Stop IDCC, Washington, DC 20402–0001

COMMITTEE ON FOREIGN AFFAIRS

EDWARD R. ROYCE, California, *Chairman*

CHRISTOPHER H. SMITH, New Jersey
ILEANA ROS-LEHTINEN, Florida
DANA ROHRABACHER, California
STEVE CHABOT, Ohio
JOE WILSON, South Carolina
MICHAEL T. McCAUL, Texas
TED POE, Texas
MATT SALMON, Arizona
DARRELL E. ISSA, California
TOM MARINO, Pennsylvania
JEFF DUNCAN, South Carolina
MO BROOKS, Alabama
PAUL COOK, California
RANDY K. WEBER SR., Texas
SCOTT PERRY, Pennsylvania
RON DeSANTIS, Florida
MARK MEADOWS, North Carolina
TED S. YOHO, Florida
CURT CLAWSON, Florida
SCOTT DesJARLAIS, Tennessee
REID J. RIBBLE, Wisconsin
DAVID A. TROTT, Michigan
LEE M. ZELDIN, New York
TOM EMMER, Minnesota

ELIOT L. ENGEL, New York
BRAD SHERMAN, California
GREGORY W. MEEKS, New York
ALBIO SIRES, New Jersey
GERALD E. CONNOLLY, Virginia
THEODORE E. DEUTCH, Florida
BRIAN HIGGINS, New York
KAREN BASS, California
WILLIAM KEATING, Massachusetts
DAVID CICILLINE, Rhode Island
ALAN GRAYSON, Florida
AMI BERA, California
ALAN S. LOWENTHAL, California
GRACE MENG, New York
LOIS FRANKEL, Florida
TULSI GABBARD, Hawaii
JOAQUIN CASTRO, Texas
ROBIN L. KELLY, Illinois
BRENDAN F. BOYLE, Pennsylvania

AMY PORTER, *Chief of Staff*   THOMAS SHEEHY, *Staff Director*
JASON STEINBAUM, *Democratic Staff Director*

————

SUBCOMMITTEE ON THE WESTERN HEMISPHERE

JEFF DUNCAN, South Carolina, *Chairman*

CHRISTOPHER H. SMITH, New Jersey
ILEANA ROS-LEHTINEN, Florida
MICHAEL T. McCAUL, Texas
MATT SALMON, Arizona
RON DeSANTIS, Florida
TED S. YOHO, Florida
TOM EMMER, Minnesota

ALBIO SIRES, New Jersey
JOAQUIN CASTRO, Texas
ROBIN L. KELLY, Illinois
GREGORY W. MEEKS, New York
ALAN GRAYSON, Florida
ALAN S. LOWENTHAL, California

CONTENTS

THE STRATEGIC IMPORTANCE OF THE WESTERN HEMISPHERE: DEFINING U.S. INTERESTS IN THE REGION

TUESDAY, FEBRUARY 3, 2015

HOUSE OF REPRESENTATIVES,
SUBCOMMITTEE ON THE WESTERN HEMISPHERE,
COMMITTEE ON FOREIGN AFFAIRS,
Washington, DC.

The committee met, pursuant to notice, at 11 o'clock a.m., in room 2172 Rayburn House Office Building, Hon. Jeff Duncan (chairman of the subcommittee) presiding.

Mr. DUNCAN. A quorum being present, the subcommittee will come to order. I will start by recognizing myself and the ranking member to present our opening statements.

Since this is our first subcommittee hearing in the 114th Congress, I will recognize members of the subcommittee that may be present after my opening statement and the ranking member's opening statement for 1 minute to present their opening remarks, introduce themselves to the committee and, if they wish to do so, they may also submit remarks for the record.

So I will now yield myself as much time as I may consume to present my opening statement. My name is Jeff Duncan. I am proud to be the subcommittee chairman on the Western Hemisphere.

I previously served as subcommittee chairman in the House Homeland Security Committee, the Subcommittee on Oversight and Management Efficiency and I am glad to be here in the Western Hemisphere Subcommittee.

So let me extend a warm welcome to the returning members of the subcommittee and I am grateful for the friendship and partnership of the ranking member, Mr. Sires, from New Jersey.

I look forward to working closely with Albio and the members of this subcommittee to help make the Department of State and USAID's action in the Western Hemisphere as efficient and effective as possible in order to advance U.S. interests in the region.

I would also like to introduce our new members and the only one on my side of the aisle is Mr. DeSantis from Florida. But the other members on the subcommittee are Ted Yoho from Florida, Tom Emmer from Minnesota—on the minority side, Mr. Joaquin Castro of Texas, Robin Kelly of Illinois, and Alan Lowenthal of California.

Each bring a wealth of experience and I am glad to have them on the subcommittee. On the majority side, our staff is Mark Walker—I guess the chief of the subcommittee staff—and Rebecca Ulrich, who formerly worked for me in my office and also on the subcommittee on Homeland Security, and Joske Bautista on the end down there working for the subcommittee.

Those are on the majority side and I hope the ranking member will introduce the—some of his staff members on the minority side because we work closely together. It is important for our members to lean on our team to make sure we are effective and if we can do that.

Today, I want to consider the strategic importance of the Western Hemisphere for U.S. interests. While our attention is often captivated by events in Asia, Europe, the Middle East, and North Africa, I do not believe that crises and firefighting should determine the level of a region's priority for the United States.

I have travelled extensively in the region—Argentina, Brazil, Canada, Colombia, Mexico, Paraguay and Peru both in my private life and also through official duties. I have got a deep affinity for the entrepreneurial people and cultures of the region.

I also firmly believe that U.S. should pay more attention to countries in the Western Hemisphere. These countries by virtue of proximity, trade, travel or culture have the ability to truly influence the United States and our lack of focus on issues right here in our own neighborhood is a disservice to the American people and to our committed partners within the region.

Although Roosevelt pledged the United States to the policy of a good neighbor in 1933, the U.S. has drifted in many ways toward benign neglect of our neighbors in Latin America and the Caribbean.

U.S. disengagement, evidenced by unsustained U.S. attention and tactical rather than strategic approaches in the region, has enabled other actors to step into the vacuum of leadership.

While countries in the Western Hemisphere do not experience the same level of chronic instability as others around the globe, this region is unique by virtue of its geography.

With no ocean separating the Americas, both threats and opportunities in Canada, the Caribbean, Latin America have a greater potential to impact the United States homeland and the American people as well as American businesses. Therefore, we must remain vigilant and truly engaged.

This year promises to be a very interesting year. With President Obama's Cuba policy shift and recent bilateral talks in Havana, this subcommittee will do its due diligence to hold the administration accountable for its actions on Cuba in order to require demonstrable results that benefit the Cuban people.

Venezuela's unstable situation, deteriorating economic conditions with major shortages and inflation at over 60 percent, declining oil production and human rights abuses also require sustained U.S. attention.

Furthermore, this year's election of a new secretary general at the Organization of American States, or the OAS, and Federal municipal elections in 13 countries in the hemisphere promise to keep us focused on advocating for transparency, adherence to the rule of law and democratic governance, as well as religious and press freedoms in the hemisphere.

Over 68,000 unaccompanied children crossed the U.S.-Mexico border last summer. This subcommittee will work to keep the administration accountable to securing the U.S.-Mexico border and preventing a second surge of migrants from Central America through wise use of American tax dollars.

Finally, the U.S. assumption of the chairmanship of the Arctic Council later this spring provides an excellent opportunity for active leadership on energy, security and freedom of navigation issues in and around the Arctic.

Since coming to Congress in 2011, I have had three simple priorities summarized by the acronym JEFF—create jobs for the American people, promote U.S. energy security and exports and return to the wisdom of our Founding Fathers.

I believe there are many ways to dig deeper into each of these areas with U.S. interests in the Western Hemisphere. First, we have seen many opportunities for U.S. businesses to engage in the region and create more American jobs in the U.S. as a result.

This region as a whole is one of the fastest growing trading partners. For instance, according to the inter-American dialogue, between 2000 and 2013, U.S. sales to Latin America more than doubled as did the region exports to U.S. markets.

In fact, the U.S. provides almost 90 percent of the $60 billion of remittance income to the region and has six free trade agreements involving 12 countries in the Western Hemisphere. This includes four individual FTAs, NAFTA, CAFTA, Dominican Republic.

Opportunities also exist for more trade with the Pacific Alliance countries of Chile, Colombia, Mexico, and Peru, which represent 36 percent of the region's economy, 50 percent of its international trade and 41 percent of all incoming foreign investment.

Additionally, with Canada, Chile, Mexico, and Peru all participating in Trans-Pacific Partnership (TPP) negotiations, I am very interested to see how TPP will impact the region.

Similarly, Chile became the 38th participant in the visa waiver program 1 year ago this month and U.S. Departments of State and Homeland Security have been in discussions with the Governments of Brazil and Uruguay about the criteria for joining the visa waiver program. That will make it easier for citizens to travel between our countries and for private sector investment and collaboration within these countries.

Second, energy opportunities abound in the region today. I am excited about the potential for U.S. energy exports from our neighbors in the hemisphere. In the 113th Congress, I authored legislation to implement the Outer Continental Shelf Trans Boundary Hydrocarbon Agreement between Mexico and the United States.

This was approved by the House and ultimately signed into law by the President. I believe we can do so much more on the energy front. The Western Hemisphere is home to nearly a third of the world's oil and the region has nearly 337 billion barrels of estimated recovery in oil, and 20 percent of the world's proven oil reserves.

The abundance of U.S. reserves in oil and natural gas and shale gas resources, the capability to export, liquefy and compress natural gas and the administration's recent announcement of offshore drilling in the Atlantic, the U.S. has many reasons to partner with like-minded countries who seek to spur economic growth, achieve energy security, and reduce energy cost.

Venezuela's dire situation, resulting impact on its Petrocaribe program, has caused 18 Central American and Caribbean nations that receive its oil on preferential terms to look elsewhere for energy security. The U.S. is a natural partner for these policies.

On January 27th, the ranking member and I co-hosted an event with Members of Congress and Caribbean leaders who were in Washington for the Caribbean Energy Security Summit.

We discussed ways to deepen energy cooperation to assist Caribbean nations in achieving energy security. Given current circumstances and the additional potential for offshore resources—resource exploration that Aruba, the Bahamas, the Dominican Republic and Trinidad are considering, U.S. businesses have a significant opportunity to engage.

Similarly, the potential for cooperation with Canada through the Keystone Pipeline and Mexico's energy sector reforms could truly take us a long way toward becoming North American energy independent if we work together to achieve that goal.

Likewise, energy opportunities in Argentina, Brazil, Colombia, and Peru could also make our hemisphere even more energy independent. And then, finally, in addition to jobs and energy I believe that we must recall the wisdom of our Founding Fathers.

In 1793, George Washington warned a young America that a reputation of weakness could lead to a loss of America's rank among nations and that if we desire to secure peace it must be known that we are at all times ready for war.

Washington also believed a uniform and well digested plan was vital to meeting these objectives. These words still ring true today—peace through strength. In the 112th Congress, I authorized legislation to address Iran's activity in the Western Hemisphere.

Passed by both houses of Congress and signed into law by President Obama, this legislation required that U.S. develop a strategy to counter Iran's activity in the region.

The recent mysterious death of Argentine prosecutor Alberto Nisman underscores the importance of being alert instead of ignoring congressional concerns, as it seems the administration has done.

Nisman bravely and boldly gave his life, holding the Government of Iran accountable for its role in the 1994 AMIA terrorist attack. Through meticulous work he exposed Iran's operations in the Western Hemisphere using Embassies, mosques, front companies, intelligence bases and sleeper cells to accomplish its purposes.

I remain deeply concerned about Iran's actions in the Western Hemisphere with evidence of a growing presence of China, North Korea, and Russia here in the Americas. We must remain ever vigilant.

With that, I turn to the ranking member, Albio Sires, for his opening statement. I look forward to hearing from our expert panel of witnesses and I thank you for being here today and I look forward to a lot of great things happening on this subcommittee. And with that, I yield to the ranking member.

Mr. SIRES. Thank you, Mr. Chairman, and congratulations to you and a warm welcome to our witnesses who have been here today.

Before I get started, I also want to recognize some of the new members that we have in our subcommittee—from Texas, Joaquin Castro, from Illinois, Robin Kelly, and from California, Alan Lowenthal.

Welcome to the committee, and I also want to recognize the former chairman who we work great—great 2 years. Nice to see that you are still interested working with us on the Western Hemisphere although you have moved on. Nice to see you, man.

And I want to express my appreciation to you, Mr. Chairman, for immediately reaching out and meeting with me to discuss how we can work together. We share many of the same concerns and aspirations and I feel encouraged by our desire to move forward in a bipartisan manner.

I look forward to working with you and the members of the subcommittee to address the numerous issues affecting our nation and neighbors in the hemisphere.

I am certain that the members of this subcommittee all agree on the strategic importance of the Western Hemisphere to U.S. interests. We may disagree on varying degree—to a varying degree on the scope and manner by which we approach certain issues.

But we ultimately want a similar peaceful, democratic, free and prosperous hemisphere—a hemisphere that upholds the Inter American Democratic Charter and respects basic human rights of free speech and assembly; a hemisphere whose citizens can elect their leaders freely and democratically without fear or coercion; a hemisphere whose citizens are safe and secure and a hemisphere whose leaders uphold the rule of law and whose citizens can aspire to some hope—to the same hopes and opportunities that we have in our country.

I have long advocated for a more focused engagement with the hemisphere. Yet, after 9/11 our focus has been on the Middle East, Asia and elsewhere. However, I believe we are finally turning the page in this regard.

While I have some clear differences and concerns with recent policy action taken in regards to Cuba, overall there are positive indications that the Western Hemisphere is finally getting the focus and attention it rightly deserves.

Late last year, the U.S. hosted the Presidents from Honduras, El Salvador and Guatemala to address the high level of violence and lack of opportunity affecting their countries.

In 2015, Mexican President Enrique Peñ a Nieto was the first leader—the first head of state to visit Washington. With oil prices falling and the economies of oil-exporting nations like Venezuela hurting, the U.S. hosted a Caribbean energy summit that could help the region diversify their dependence from Petrocaribe.

Additionally, the administration's recent announcement committing $1 billion for Central America is a significant step. If approved, it will go far in helping improve the safety, security and economic well-being of the region that is amongst the most violent in the world and a pathway for illicit drugs bound for the United States.

For detractors that doubt the strategic relevance of the region to the United States, I need only to remind them of the humanitarian crisis that erupted on our southern border. Thousands of young women and children fled their country escaping violence or were lured by coyotes with false hope of a broken U.S. immigration system.

It is also but a down payment compared to the cost of doing nothing, and yet this issue merely underscores lingering problems in terms of weak institutions, corruption and poverty. Indeed, together with changing demographics and economic trends, there will be many challenges facing the hemisphere.

But there are also many opportunities that will serve to integrate us further. More than half of the U.S. immigrants come from the Western Hemisphere. Geographic proximity has forged strong and robust commercial ties.

In spite of an increasing Chinese presence, U.S. trade with the region was more than three times that of China in 2013. Canada is our number one trading partner and Mexico is a close third.

Today, we are witnessing a global economic adjustment with a decline in oil and commodity prices. China's economy is cooling and with it is demand for natural resources from key markets in South America.

Countries that benefited from high commodity prices will face difficult decisions while importers will be given some breathing room. On the other hand, the U.S. economy is rebounding alongside a North American energy transformation with broad geopolitical implications. Elsewhere, there is a combination of promise and concern.

Mexico has come a long way but the context behind the death and disappearance of 43 university students has revealed shortcomings in dealings with corruption and violence.

Brazil and Argentina are countries with which our relations can be much improved. The sudden tragic death of Argentina prosecutor Alberto Nisman was a shock. But I implore Argentine authorities to commit themselves to fully investigate the matter and continue his work to bring those behind the horrific 1994 AMIA bombing to justice. And in Colombia, our strongest regional ally, there is a potential to end a 50-year-old conflict.

While I have many reservations about trusting the FARC, I stand completely committed to supporting the people of Colombia as they move forward and I believe the United States should do the same.

I look forward to hearing from our witnesses and working with the chairman and our members to address these issues. Thank you.

Mr. DUNCAN. I want to thank the ranking member and he is exactly correct that we are going to work well together and I value our relationship.

I heard one thing that he said. I wanted to make sure I clarify. I heard him say China was our best trading partner. Canada is our largest and best trading partner. That was in his notes and I am not sure if what he said but what I heard. But I just want to make sure that—that Canada is our largest trading partner and I think that is what you intended to say.

Mr. SIRES. My accent.

Mr. DUNCAN. Yes, sir. What I would like to do is, because this is our first meeting I would like to give all the members a chance for 1 minute to introduce yourself.

If you want to state, you know, your goal as a subcommittee member or maybe what your focus is so we all can get to know each other just a little bit better and the audience can as well.

So I will start by recognizing the first member is Mr. DeSantis from Florida for 1 minute.

Mr. DeSantis. Well, thank you, Mr. Chairman. I look forward to our work over these next 2 years. We have some important things that we need to tackle, most recently with what the administration has done with Cuba policy.

Here you have a regime that was really struggling with their patrons in Moscow and Caracas, roiled by lower energy prices, and this is essentially a unilateral concession, a huge lifeline to the Castro government.

I think it was a major mistake. We worked very hard on this committee last Congress to stand up for the people in Venezuela who were chafing under the Maduro regime. I think the administration has had a tepid response to that.

Finally, there has been some action taken in the last few days but I think we have got to unequivocally stand with those freedom fighters in Venezuela.

And I think, finally, we do have to be concerned with the rise of rogue state actors in our hemisphere and we have seen that with Iran. We have seen it with North Korea and we also have, of course, rival states like Russia and China who are seeking to have a foothold here. So I look forward to it and congratulations on your chairmanship.

Mr. Duncan. Thank you. The Chair will recognize Mr. Meeks from New York for 1 minute.

Mr. Meeks. Thank you, Mr. Chairman, and I also want to thank my good friend, Ranking Member Sires, and I am delighted to be serving on this subcommittee once again and I look forward to working with you on a region that must be a top priority for our nation.

As a New York representative, I am mindful at all times of the benefits of harmonious and thriving relationships with the region. Canada borders my state and our partnership is deep and thriving.

Top energy—Canada is our top energy supplier, top trading partner. The list is long, and I know my colleagues to the south can say similar things about Mexico. In all my years on this committee I do not recall a more promising time in hemispheric developments.

While it is true that we still have many intractable problems to tackle, it is also true that today we will be discussing developments that not long ago seemed out of reach. In my estimation we are finally witnessing the dismantling of deeply entrenched Cold War vestiges.

When I travel to Colombia, most of the people I meet have known nothing but civil war conflict that has raged in the nation for over 50 years. Now, the world's longest lasting civil war is on the brink of peace as the FARC guerrillas and the Government of Colombia engaged in talks in Havana.

A little over a year after making the Colombia embargo permanent, speaking at the White House to a room full of over 200 Latin American diplomats, President Kennedy proposed the Alliance for Progressive Initiative.

It was a 10-year planned partnership with regional governments to facilitate social and economic advancement in Latin America to, in his words, "build a hemisphere where all men can hope for a sustainable standard of living and all can live out their lives in dignity and freedom," and at that unveiling JFK made an acknowledgement that would ring true for some decades to come when he said, "Let me be the first to admit that we North Americans have not always grasped the significance of this common mission."

So I know, Mr. Chairman, that in just a couple of months at the upcoming Summit of the Americas our nation will demonstrate that we Americans do fully grasp the significance of our commonality with our neighbors in the region and I am confident that recent changes by the Obama administration to U.S.-Cuba policy and other forward-looking policy changes toward Latin America and the Caribbean will put America more in sync with our regional allies.

Let me just say this as I close that I am looking forward to hearing from our witnesses today about the significance of the monumental changes on the horizon for our region and how we might embrace and advance a common agenda in the months ahead.

I have read your testimony and I know that you have an expansive wealth of knowledge to gain and I have to gain from your knowledge. I look forward to hearing your testimony. Thank you.

Mr. DUNCAN. Thank you, Mr. Meeks.

The Chair will recognize Mr. Emmer from Minnesota for 1 minute.

Mr. EMMER. Thank you, Mr. Chair. My name is Tom Emmer and I am from Minnesota. I want to thank you and Ranking Member Sires.

I am excited to serve on this subcommittee because of the strategic importance of the region to the United States and the entire world. Serving as a major trade, energy and economic region, the Western Hemisphere offers numerous emerging opportunities to the United States today and for the decades to come.

I am looking forward to learning—listening and learning from my colleagues and meeting and working with leaders from the region to continue to advance more transparent and open cooperation between the U.S. and members of the Western Hemisphere and I look forward to working specifically on issues of energy, trade, diplomatic relations and security during the 114th Congress.

Again, I am honored to be part of this subcommittee and I can't wait to get to work.

Thank you, Mr. Chairman. I yield back.

Mr. DUNCAN. Thank you. I am taking in order members' arrival. So Mr. Yoho from Florida is recognized for 1 minute.

Mr. YOHO. Thank you, Mr. Chairman, and congratulations on chairing this committee. I look forward to it and working with you on this.

I think this is a great first hearing that will let new members—new members to the subcommittee like myself really get an overview of the Western Hemisphere and the implications in the region that it has for our national security and economy.

You know, I grew up in—I was born in Minnesota but I have lived in Florida 52 of my 60 years and it is home to me and I have had the pleasure of working as a large animal veterinarian in Florida for 30 years, and we deal a lot with the farmers and ranchers we have gotten to know and the extension of the agricultural sector into the South America mainly.

And I look forward to bolstering these and I look forward to strengthening our relationships in the whole Latin American and Western Hemisphere and the security in the region, I think, is utmost that we pay attention.

I have got members in the—family members in the Coast Guard and I hear daily of stories of the narco trade, the illegal immigration, human trafficking and I look forward to bringing some common sense resolutions to that to make our nation stronger as we bolster our relationship with those countries; and I look forward to hearing from the experts here and I know we are going to have a productive 2 years, and thank you.

Mr. DUNCAN. I thank the gentleman.

The Chair will recognize the former chairman of the Subcommittee on Western Hemisphere, now the chairman of the Asia and the Pacific Subcommittee, Mr. Salmon, for an opening statement of 1 minute.

Mr. SALMON. Thank you, Mr. Chairman.

My top priority is just to do whatever I can to make you look good and my second priority is just do whatever the gentlewoman from Florida tells me to do.

The third thing is I really am very, very concerned about a phenomena we saw last year that really had strong implications in my state with regard to Guatemala and El Salvador and the whole Central America problem with unaccompanied minors at the border.

I think we are going to see it again in a very big way, and we have never really done anything to resolve it. The House worked its will last August and passed legislation which the Senate never took up.

But it hasn't gone away. We don't know exactly why it tapered off. A lot of people think it was just weather. But the violence in Guatemala, Honduras, El Salvador continues. The drug trafficking and the gangs that bolster that drug trafficking, the coyotes—all of those things have not gone away.

There are great things happening in the Western Hemisphere—great exciting things, and you have noted a lot of them. But there are some real challenges too and they are showing up right at our door and causing some real serious issues within our country and I hope we get a handle on it.

I hope it is something that we intend to focus some attention on, because, as we went to the border of Guatemala and Mexico and saw first hand with General Kelly what was going on right there in terms of drug trafficking, people trafficking, gun trafficking, it hadn't gone away and I really hope that we focus some attention and ultimately address it as a Congress and try to get it fixed. Thank you.

Mr. DUNCAN. I thank the gentleman for his leadership. I am just really following up and continuing your great work. So the Chair will recognize Mr. Castro from Texas for 1 minute.

Mr. CASTRO. Thank you, Chairman. It is an honor to serve on this subcommittee. I think the task for us in the years ahead is to continue to develop the infrastructures for diplomacy, economic development and cooperation within the Western Hemisphere.

There are things that happen in Latin America that if they happened in other parts of the world this body, the Congress, and the United States would respond much more swiftly and much more strongly, and I will use the example that Chairman Salmon pointed out.

We had a subcommittee hearing on all the kids that came from Central America. But there was never a full committee hearing on that situation. That needs to change in the future. We need to attend to this region much better than we have before.

Mr. DUNCAN. I thank the gentleman.

Mr. Lowenthal from California is recognized for 1 minute.

Mr. LOWENTHAL. Thank you, Chairman Duncan and Ranking Member Sires. I want to thank you both for holding this important hearing focusing on the Western Hemisphere and its relationship to our U.S. interests.

As a first time member of this subcommittee and as a former legislator for southern California and also as a former professor at Cal State Long Beach where I had the very good fortune of spending a year sabbatical at the University of Yucatan, I am really pleased to be focusing much more on our relationship with Mexico and Central America and parts of the region, especially since so many of the families in my region, in my district, are directly impacted by events that occur in the region.

I am here to learn, as the chairman asked me, also what would be my focus. As I pointed out, I am an educator. I would like to see, with 28 percent poverty, how we work with the region in terms of educational opportunities, how—what are the successes in education.

I am also concerned about our collaboration on the energy and climate partnership, on clean energy and I would like to understand what that means and how that works; and I, too, would like to understand more about unaccompanied minors, both the causes and potential solutions than what we have and I thank you for holding this hearing.

Mr. DUNCAN. Thank you, Mr. Lowenthal.

And the Chair will now recognize the former chairman of the full committee and a mentor of mine, Ms. Ros-Lehtinen from Florida.

Ms. ROS-LEHTINEN. Well, thank you so much, Mr. Chairman. It is a pleasure and a privilege to serve on your subcommittee. I think it is important to note that, according to financial reports, U.S. producers export three times more to Latin America than they do to China.

Thirteen out of 17 Latin American countries import more goods from our country—from the United States than from any other country in the world.

So even those countries with strong anti-American rhetoric silently continue to do business with us as sources for trade and investment and that is where we need to take a real deep look at our region.

As we have seen with the misguided secret negotiations with Cuba, our foreign policy seems to have left democracy and human rights as distant priorities. This is an unacceptable premise for our country, the greatest democracy in the world.

Our policies toward our hemisphere must champion democratic freedoms and fundamental rights whether it is my native homeland of Cuba, Venezuela, Nicaragua, Ecuador, Bolivia, and I know, Mr. Chairman, that under your leadership this subcommittee will continue to do our investigation about Iran's destabilizing role in Latin America; and I know that we will look at the murder of Alberto Nisman, the AMIA Jewish Community Center prosecutor, and the mystery surrounding his death.

So thank you, Mr. Chairman. I can't think of anyone who could be a better chairman except, of course, Mr. Salmon—both equally good.

Mr. DUNCAN. Well, nobody could beat Matt Salmon. But anyway, thank you, and the last member to be recognized, Ms. Kelly from Illinois, for 1 minute.

Ms. KELLY. Thank you, Mr. Chair. I am both thrilled to be on Foreign Affairs and also on this committee. I am very interested in learning as much as I can and, also, I want us to develop ways we can partner in peace and fair trade that we can all benefit from no matter the country.

This committee was of particular interest because, representing Chicago, I have a significant Mexican and Polish population. Also, as a Chicago rep with crime pipelines that have links to Latin America, I am very concerned about transnational crime, drug trafficking and illicit finance. Those are both big concerns.

And, lastly, I am interested in finding ways we can continue to find productive and positive ways to build our relationship with Cuba and its people.

Thank you.

Mr. DUNCAN. I thank the members, and from what I am hearing we are going to have a very active and beneficial time to make us all better congressmen and make the committee effective; and make the United States a better partner in the region.

So we can't do that at every committee hearing but so I need to say that pursuant to Committee Rule 7 members of the subcommittee will be permitted to submit written statements to be included in the official hearing record.

Without objection, the hearing record will remain open for 5 days to allow statements, questions and extraneous materials for the record subject to the length and limitation in the rules.

So now it is a pleasure of mine to introduce our distinguished panel today and the first panelist is Dr. Shannon O'Neil. Dr. O'Neil is a senior fellow for Latin American studies on the Council on Foreign Relations.

Her expertise includes U.S.-Latin American relations, trade, energy and immigration. She also directed CFR's independent task force on North America, ''Time for a New Focus''—I think there is a copy of the book at your desk—as well as an independent task force on ''U.S.-Latin America Relations: A New Direction for a New Reality.''

Dr. O'Neil holds an MA in international relations from Yale and a Ph.D. in government from Harvard.

Our second panelist is Ms. Bonnie Glick. Ms. Glick served as senior vice president—serves currently as senior vice president for Global Connect Division at Meridian International Center.

Prior to joining Meridian, Ms. Glick served 12 years as a U.S. diplomat in the Department of State. She served in the U.S. Embassy in Managua, Nicaragua and in the period immediately after the electoral defeat of the Sandinistas. It is an interesting—I would like to talk with you more about that.

Ms. Glick also holds an MA in international affairs from Columbia University, an MBA from the Robert H. Smith School of Business at University of Maryland.

Our third panelist, Dr. Evan Ellis—Dr. Evan Ellis is a research professor in Latin American studies and an accomplished author. He has given testimony on Chinese activities in Latin America to the U.S Congress, and has discussed his work regarding China and other external sectors in Latin America on various media outlets.

Dr. Ellis holds a Ph.D. in political science from Purdue with a specialization in comparative politics.

And our last panelist, Mr. Eric Farnsworth—Mr. Farnsworth is vice president of the Council of the Americas and Americas Society. Mr. Farnsworth began his career in Washington with the U.S. Department of State. He also served as senior advisor to the White House Special Envoy for the Americas.

He holds an MBA in international relations from Princeton's Woodrow Wilson School and we are glad you guys are here. I have enjoyed getting to know Eric and look forward to talking with him more.

So we have got a lighting system. We are going to recognize each of the panelists for 5 minutes. That also goes for the committee.

When we get to the question period we are going to adhere to the 5-minute rule, and I will try to adhere to that as closely as possible due to the essence of time. So if you hear a light tapping and not a—then that means wrap it up with a sentence.

I don't want to go to the second part of that. So we would like to try to stay on time. So before I recognize you to provide your testimony I am going to continue to—I have already explained that.

So after our witnesses testify we will have 5 minutes to ask questions and so, Dr. O'Neil, I am going to start with you. It is kind of strange how the committee has been set up. Usually it runs the other way in recognizing them but we are going to start on the right.

Dr. O'Neil, you are recognized for 5 minutes.

STATEMENT OF SHANNON K. O'NEIL, PH.D., SENIOR FELLOW FOR LATIN AMERICA STUDIES, COUNCIL ON FOREIGN RELATIONS

Ms. O'NEIL. Great. Good morning. So Mr. Chairman, Ranking Member and members of the subcommittee, thank you for the invitation to testify today and I am grateful for the subcommittee's interest on the Council on Foreign Relations' Independent Task Force on North America, and I am pleased to have the opportunity to discuss it and the strategic importance of North America for U.S. interests.

And if it would be acceptable to the chair, I would like to have the entirety of the referenced task force report entered into the record.

Now, home to nearly 500 million people living in three vibrant democracies, North America today is an economic global powerhouse. At over $20 trillion, the three nations of Canada, Mexico, and the United States account for over a quarter of global GDP.

Moreover, North America is increasingly interdependent as geography, markets, policies, the choices of millions of individuals and the choices of hundreds and thousands of companies have transformed it into one of the most integrated regions in the world.

And given these deep and indelible links, a stronger North America can only enhance U.S. competitiveness, U.S. security and well-being and it can also bolster U.S. influence globally.

Now, in my time here I want to talk about two opportunities in particular that stand out for areas of cooperation and these are energy and economic competitiveness.

Starting with energy—never before have the energy prospects of these three nations been so dynamic as they have been transformed by new energy finds in the three nations, by new technologies and by new rules, particularly in Mexico, that are together unleashing an unanticipated potential.

An increasing energy production so far has brought jobs, it has boosted economic growth and it has lowered prices for industrial and individual consumers in all three nations.

Now, as each of these three countries undergo their own changes and transformations, energy should become a fundamental pillar for the North American partnership. Greater regional cooperation and integration will boost economic, geopolitical, and environmental benefits for these three nations.

To truly harness North America's energy promise, the United States should work closely with its neighbors to integrate North America's energy markets. So this will involve significant investment in resources, in cross border infrastructure and electricity grids, so physically linking North America's energy fields, refineries and markets.

It will also mean developing regional energy strategies and environmental standards, coordinating on issues such as regulations, safety procedures, energy efficiency guidelines and technologies for lower carbon energy.

Common efforts like these will better ensure the three countries benefit from the potential economic gains while also reaching environmental and carbon objectives.

Now, let me turn to North America's economic potential. Now, over the past two decades North America's economic ties have deepened dramatically by virtually all measures.

Today, each of these nations is the others' largest trading partners with intra-regional trade of over $1 trillion a year, and as important is the changed nature of this trade, reflecting the rise of a truly regional production platform.

So rather than sending each other finished products the United States, Mexico and Canada today trade in pieces and parts. So this

14

back and forth along assembly lines, between plants and between these countries in the making of every car, every plane, every flat screen TV or computer it means for every item that is imported from Mexico to the United States, 40 percent of its value on average, was actually made in the United States and for Canada the number is 25 percent.

And it is precisely through this integration of joint production of goods that the United States, Canada, and Mexico have become more efficient and competitive together than they would have been alone.

And as this new Congress begins its work, made in North America should be a foundation of U.S. policy. So this means working toward the free unimpeded movement of goods and services across North America's common borders.

This will require reducing non-tariff barriers, revising rules of origin, mutually recognizing or harmonizing differing regulations, expanding preclearance or other proven programs for trusted travellers, and investing in border infrastructure necessary to speed trade and travel.

It also means prioritizing and completing free trade agreements with which the United States, Canada, and Mexico are all part, specifically today the Trans-Pacific Partnership, and it should mean incorporating our North American neighbors and other free trade agreements we consider including the Trans-Atlantic Trade and Investment Partnership, or TTIP, with Europe.

Now, the costs of not engaging our neighbors are even higher than they have been in the past. In a world of regional blocs, deepening U.S. ties with its economic allies and particularly its neighbors will help maintain our national competitiveness, and America's dream of energy self-sufficiency depends, too, on its neighbors, on linking energy and electricity grids to ensure safe, stable and resilient supplies.

The United States is already a global superpower but with its neighbors it could extend its reach even further, and so I would ask you as policy makers to put North America at the forefront of your imaginations and, importantly, on your agendas.

Thank you.

[The prepared statement of Ms. O'Neil follows:]

COUNCILon
FOREIGN
RELATIONS

February 3, 2015

The Strategic Importance of North America to U.S. Interests

Prepared statement by
Shannon O'Neil
Senior Fellow for Latin America Studies
Council on Foreign Relations

Before the
House Foreign Affairs Subcommittee on the Western Hemisphere
United States House of Representatives
1st Session, *114*th Congress

Hearing on The Strategic Importance of the Western Hemisphere: Defining U.S. Interests in the Region

Mr. Chairman, Ranking Member, and Members of the Subcommittee: Thank you for the invitation to testify today. I am grateful for the Subcommittee's interest in the Council on Foreign Relation's Independent Task Force on North America's report and pleased to have this opportunity to discuss the strategic importance of North America for U.S. interests. If it would be acceptable to the Chair, I'd like the entirety of the referenced task force report to be entered into the record. As always, I am eager to hear your advice and counsel.

North America today is a global economic powerhouse, home to almost five hundred million people living in three vibrant democracies. Together the three nations account for over 26 percent of global GDP. Totaling roughly $20 trillion, their combined economies outpace the European Union in economic production. And though the United States makes up the majority of the economic weight (in terms of GDP and as the home to almost a third of the world's largest companies), both Canada and Mexico rank among the top fifteen largest global economies. North America is also one of the most economically dynamic regions of the world today—the World Bank predicts the region will outperform average global GDP growth in 2015.

Because of geography, markets, and the choices of millions of individuals and thousands of companies, North America has become one of the most integrated and interdependent regions in the world. Sharing 7,500 miles of peaceful borders, Canada and Mexico now play vital roles in the United States' stability, security, and prosperity. It is time to build on past work and advance this partnership to a new stage. If the three North American countries deepen their integration and cooperation, they have the potential to improve the standards of living of their citizens and to shape world affairs for generations to come.

Several recent developments make a North American vision particularly attractive. These include advantageous demographics, a shared skilled labor force, and recent economic reforms in Mexico. Today, I want to focus on two particular areas of opportunity: energy and economic competitiveness.

Energy

North America's energy landscape is changing dramatically. In 2005, net imports made up 60 percent of U.S. fuel consumption. The growing gap between the United States' energy demand and domestic supply added to worries about the U.S. trade deficit, economy, and security.[1] Today, U.S. oil import dependence has dropped to less than one-third of total consumption, and the country is shifting rapidly from energy scarcity to opportunity. Rising shale oil and gas production in the United States, increasing exploration and development in the Canadian oil sands, and landmark reforms in Mexico's energy sector have led many experts to predict the potential—especially for North American natural gas—for self-sufficiency and even surplus in the coming decades. The growing production and regional diversification of energy sources will boost North America's energy security and competitiveness.

As this energy renaissance evolves, the decisions the United States, Canada, and Mexico make about energy will have major implications for their own and their neighbors' economies, national security, foreign policy, and environments. As a result, energy should become a fundamental pillar of North America's new partnership.

One area for cooperation is the integration of energy matrices and the strengthening of continental energy infrastructure. The United States should work with its neighbors to increase energy connections. From gas and oil pipelines to electricity grids, deeper integration of cross-border infrastructure would make supply more stable and resilient, benefiting companies, workers, and communities more broadly.

North America can also lead the way in energy efficiency. Harmonizing environmental standards and policies, and cooperating in the development and diffusion of technologies to promote energy conservation and lessen carbon costs should also be part of developing a regional energy strategy.

Economic Competitiveness

Over the past two decades, North America's economic ties have deepened dramatically by almost all measures; they have the potential to develop even further. The region's trade grew from less than $300 billion in 1993 to over $1.1 trillion in 2013, making the United States, Canada, and Mexico each other's most important trading partners.[ii] Today, the United States exports more than four times as much to Mexico and Canada as it does to China and more than twice as much as to the European Union.[iii] Cross-border investment also skyrocketed, rising fivefold since 1993 to total an investment stock of some $791 billion by 2012.[iv] While the majority comprises U.S. foreign direct investment in its neighbors, $333 billion of it reflects Mexican and Canadian investments in the United States—particularly in the manufacturing, insurance, banking, and consumer sectors.[v]

The type of trade in North America has also changed—shifting from primarily finished goods, to pieces and parts that move back and forth across borders as part of regional supply chains. A study by the National Bureau of Economic Research reported that on average 40 percent of the value of products imported from Mexico and 25 percent of those from Canada actually come from the United States; the comparable input percentage with the rest of the world is about 4 percent.[vi] This means that of the $280 billion in goods that the United States imported from Mexico in 2013, some $112 billion of the value was created in the United States; for the $332 billion that the United States imported from Canada, the value created in the United States was $83 billion. In comparison, less than $20 billion of the value from the $440 billion of U.S. imports from China came from U.S. workers.[vii]

A large part of North America's economic dynamism stems from its interdependence, which accelerated following the 1993 North American Free Trade Agreement (NAFTA). As the continent has moved closer to becoming a joint innovation, design, production, and service platform, the United States, Canada, and Mexico have become more efficient and competitive together. This has mattered for companies and workers—supporting profits and employment. A recent Peterson Institute for International Economics report estimates that U.S. exports to Canada and Mexico supported 2.6 million and 1.9 million U.S. jobs respectively.[viii]

"Made in North America" should be a foundation for U.S. foreign policy. This means working toward the free and unimpeded movement of goods and services across North America's common borders.

Today there are two main types of barriers. The first are physical limitations at the border. Investment in infrastructure lags far behind the increased flows of people, cars, trucks, and goods, hindering the competitiveness of North America as a region. More investment is needed in auxiliary roads, rail infrastructure, bridges, airports, and ports that enable cross-border flows and then connect them with the larger U.S. economy. Congress has an important role to play in making infrastructure investment a priority and passing funding legislation. In addition, it should support the expansion of successful preclearance programs that expedite the movement of trusted goods and travelers across borders, as these too speed commerce.

Along with physical barriers are regulatory and bureaucratic ones. Rules of origin, non-tariff barriers, and multiple customs filings slow or impede regional trade. The U.S. government, working closely with the private sector, should review and revise NAFTA's rules of origin provisions to lower the cost for companies operating in the region. The United States should address divergent regulations, working toward mutual recognition or harmonization through the U.S.-Mexico High-Level Regulatory Council and the U.S.-Canada Regulatory Cooperation Council. Bureaucratically, the United States should accelerate plans to introduce a North American "single window" customs system that eliminates multiple filings. Together these changes would streamline regional commerce further, benefiting producers and workers in all three nations.

As NAFTA reaches its twentieth anniversary, there is much to applaud in terms of advances in trade, investment, and productivity. By expanding regional exchanges in goods and services, boosting cross-border investment, deepening the integration of production processes, it helped maintain and create many jobs, while also producing higher quality goods at lower prices, benefiting North American businesses, workers, and consumers.

Still, the gains have not been spread evenly. NAFTA left some better and some worse off, and it has yet to lead to the promised economic convergence between the three nations. In part, these shortcomings stem from the initial overselling of the trade agreement. But they also reflect the need for a twenty-first century upgrade in the economic relationship between the three partners—addressing the issues that were left off the table (energy and the movement of people, among others), as well as the new issues that have emerged or transformed over the last two decades, from intellectual property rights to regulatory coherence, and from e-commerce to cyber security. The Trans-Pacific Partnership (TPP) negotiations, of which both Canada and Mexico are a part, provide an opportunity to address many of these limitations, strengthening the North American production platform.

Finally, North America increasingly shares a workforce, as companies and corporations make products and provide services across all three countries. Within these integrated supply chains, employees in one country depend on the performance of those in another; together, they contribute to the quality and competitiveness of final products that are sold regionally or globally.

Led by the United States, the region boasts many of the top academic institutions in the world. But ensuring quality education at the elementary and secondary levels has been a struggle—the Program for International Student Assessment (PISA) test scores put Mexico at the bottom of the thirty-four Organization for Economic Cooperation and Development (OECD) countries in reading, science, and math, and the United States mired in the middle. Only Canada makes it into the top five in each category.

Given the interlacing of North America's workforces, the United States should work with Canada and Mexico to develop a regional education and innovation strategy. This strategy should include a diversity of public and private education and technical training programs, incorporate new technologies, increase affordability, expand skills certification, and connect students to private employers. It should also promote regional research through professional academic exchanges and the creation of a North American network of laboratories for basic research.

Conclusion

Unlike so many U.S. foreign policy priorities that strive to reduce differences and hostilities, North American relations focus primarily on identifying and building upon similarities and shared interests. One promising areas is energy, where the changes occurring are already giving North America a global competitive advantage, and where further coordination can ensure reliable, affordable, and environmentally sustainable energy production, strengthening each country and North America as a whole. A second vital area is economic competitiveness. As the United States works to jumpstart its own economic growth, North American production provides one of the most promising paths forward. And the benefits of a stronger and more integrated region extend beyond energy and commerce, influencing basic security, stability, and prosperity. Working more closely with Canada and Mexico, the United States today has an opportunity to promote a positive agenda, benefiting citizens in all three nations.

[i]. U.S. Energy Information Administration, "AEO2014 Early Release Overview," U.S. Energy Information Administration, December 16, 2013, http://www.eia.gov/forecasts/aeo/er/early_production.cfm.

[ii]. U.S. Census Bureau, "U.S. Trade in Goods with Mexico," U.S. Census Bureau, accessed March 19, 2014, http://www.census.gov/foreign-trade/balance/c2010.html; U.S. Census Bureau, "U.S. Trade in Goods with Canada," U.S. Census Bureau, accessed March 19, 2014, http://www.census.gov/foreign-trade/balance/c1220.html.

[iii]. U.S. Census Bureau, "U.S. Trade in Goods with China," U.S. Census Bureau, accessed December 4, 2013, http://www.census.gov/foreign-trade/balance/c5700.html; U.S. Census Bureau, "U.S. Trade in Goods with European Union," U.S. Census Bureau, accessed December 4, 2013, http://www.census.gov/foreign-trade/balance/c0003.html.

[iv]. Organization for Economic Cooperation and Development, "FDI Positions by Partner Country," accessed August 11, 2014, http://www.oecd.org/corporate/mne/statistics.htm.

[v]. Bureau of Economic Analysis, "Foreign Direct Investment in the U.S.: Balance of Payments and Direct Investment Position Data," U.S. Department of Commerce, accessed July 3, 2014, https://www.bea.gov/international/di1fdibal.htm.

[vi]. Robert Koopman, William Powers, Zhi Wang, and Shang-Jin Wei, "Give Credit Where Credit is Due: Tracing Value Added In Global Production Chains," National Bureau of Economic Research, p. 38, September 2010, http://www.nber.org/papers/w16426.pdf.

[vii]. U.S. Census Bureau, "U.S. Trade in Goods with Mexico," U.S. Census Bureau, accessed March 19, 2014, http://www.census.gov/foreign-trade/balance/c2010.html; U.S. Census Bureau, "U.S. Trade in Goods with Canada," U.S. Census Bureau, accessed April 28, 2014, https://www.census.gov/foreign-trade/balance/c1220.html#2013; U.S. Census Bureau, "U.S. Trade in Goods with China," U.S. Census Bureau, accessed March 19, 2014, http://www.census.gov/foreign-trade/balance/c1220.html.

[viii]. Gary Clyde Hufbauer, Cathleen Cimino, and Tyler Moran, "NAFTA at 20: Misleading Charges and Positive Achievements," Peterson Institute for International Economics, p. 2, May 2014, http://www.piie.com/publications/pb/pb14-13.pdf.

Mr. DUNCAN. And the Chair will recognize Ms. Glick for 5 minutes.

STATEMENT OF MS. BONNIE GLICK, SENIOR VICE PRESIDENT, GLOBALCONNECT DIVISION, MERIDIAN INTERNATIONAL CENTER

Ms. GLICK. Mr. Chairman, Ranking Member and members of the committee, thank you for the invitation to testify today. I am here representing Meridian International Center, a Washington, DC-based nonprofit that focuses on the promotion of global leadership through international engagement.

I also come in my capacity as a former executive of the IBM Corporation and as a former Foreign Service officer. By crossing sectors from public to private to nonprofit, I have seen the impact that U.S. engagement in the Western Hemisphere can have and today I will focus my remarks on the economic importance of remaining engaged with our neighbors to the south.

I would like to say that the importance of Latin America is best summed up in a Spanish word, intercambio. An intercambio is an interchange, kind of a clumsy word in English but quite elegant in what it implies.

We no longer teach or train our neighbors. It is no longer a one-way street. The intercambios that exist today are really the super-highways of information and knowledge exchange. All parties involved benefit and this leads to economic growth.

Emerging market country strategies have for years focused on moving up the value chain in terms of their exports, producing higher valued goods and services. Several Latin American countries' economies have seen successes that mirror the Asian Tigers. I will call these the Latin American Tigres.

When U.S. companies are looking for countries in which to invest, countries where there are good prospects for growth, long term return on their investments and strong partnerships, it makes sense to look toward Latin America.

The global economy calls for the diversification of investments and successful countries where we have used our bilateral government-to-government relationships based mostly on foreign assistance and dependency have morphed into countries where businesses can have relationships based on mutual interests and growth.

Colombia is an example of U.S. foreign assistance that worked. Today, Colombia is a thriving democracy and an example of an economic and financial powerhouse in the region. Medellin, once the drug capital of the world, is now one of the leading financial and industrial centers in Latin America.

This once profoundly dangerous city is now listed by Forbes Magazine as one of the 10 best cities in the world for international retirees. Colombia is now a Latin Tigre. Another example of its success is in the oil industry. Colombia's oil giant, Ecopetrol, is a para statal company that is well managed with revenues of nearly $38 billion.

The current downturn in oil prices has certainly impacted Ecopetrol, but its asset base and reserves will allow it to weather the economic storm.

Colombia lets the world know that it is open for business. Indeed, in 2014 it rose from spot number 53 to number 34 on the World Bank's ease of doing business index.

Brazil is the biggest player in South America. Its period of prosperity when the BRIC was the preeminent force of nature in emerging markets began in the late '90s with the government decision to privatize some of Brazil's Government-owned enterprises. Moving massive and poorly performing industries into private hands led to sustained growth of around 5 percent per year.

However, the Brazilian Government has often looked at the economic miracle of Brazil as a means to provide expanded, and sometimes unaffordable, services to the country's large population.

Brazil has now become a burdensome place to do business, and it is near the bottom of the list of the World Bank's ease of doing business index in the unenviable 120th spot. But international investors, including Americans, will not flee from Brazil.

Brazil has the largest offshore oil discovery on Earth. The deepwater offshore exploration and production will continue and expand in the decades to come. Brazil's oil industry, with the opportunities for investment by American oil companies, means that U.S. oil can diversify their holdings and can weather global economic storms with less risk.

This mitigated risk allows those same American companies to expand operations and employment very directly in the United States and in other operations abroad.

U.S. equipment manufacturers can generate significant sales, in turn boosting our own economy and stimulating job creation at home. For many years, Chile held a role as the darling among Latin American countries that is slowly being supplanted by Columbia.

Chile remains a financial and mining industry giant in the region, but the newly returned presidency of Michelle Bachelet has many an industry seeing the return of more socialist tendencies that are less business friendly. The new tax regime will be the first test of the global business community's patience with Chile.

Today, I would like to discuss briefly Mexico in the context of its multilateral role in the newly formed trade bloc known as the Pacific Alliance.

Mexico wields a tremendous amount of influence due in no small part to its proximity to the world's economic golden goose—us. Mexico currently sits at spot number 39 on the World Bank's ease of doing business index and Mexico is the lynchpin country forming the Pacific Alliance, as mentioned by the chairman—a free trade area comprised of Mexico, Colombia, Peru, and Chile.

It was formed in 2013 as a counterbalance to the Mercosur trade bloc. The Pacific Alliance counterweight, though, packs quite a punch. In its first year, the Pacific Alliance's trade with external partners outpaced Mercosur's, and this pattern appears likely to continue.

This newly formed trade bloc of Latin American Tigres shows great promise in the global economy with average annual growth of 4.2 percent. We should not relax, however, and think that U.S. companies can sit back and reap the rewards from relationships that are driven by geography.

The name of the emerging trade bloc gives clues as to its orientation. The Pacific Alliance means a pivot to Asia. Indeed, the superhighway I referenced earlier is every bit a present day reality.

American businesses must fasten their seatbelts for the ride. Businesses should remain engaged so as not to lose market share to China and the Asian Tigers. Engagement, investment, collaboration, partnership, and active participation all ensure that our businesses will grow, will continue to maintain a footprint in the most stable region of the world outside North America, and will create jobs and investment opportunities for Americans at home and abroad.

I thank you very much for your time today.

[The prepared statement of Ms. Glick follows:]

BONNIE GLICK

SENIOR VICE PRESIDENT, MERIDIAN INTERNATIONAL CENTER

HOUSE COMMITTEE ON FOREIGN AFFAIRS

Tuesday, February 3, 2015

"The Strategic Importance of the Western Hemisphere: Defining U.S. Interests in the Region"

Mr. Chairman, Ranking Member, and Members of the Committee: Thank you for the invitation to testify today. I am grateful for the Committee's interest in hearing about the Strategic Importance of the Western Hemisphere and Defining U.S. Interests in the Region. I am here in my capacity as the Senior Vice President of Meridian International Center, a Washington, DC-based non-profit that focuses on promotion of global leadership through international engagement. We connect public and private leaders at all levels to promote collaboration in solving global problems. I also come in my capacity as a former executive of the IBM Corporation, another global entity also focused on solving some of the world's toughest problems through the application of "Smarter" solutions. I spent the past twelve years with IBM before joining to Meridian in May, and much of my time was spent in Latin America. Prior to that, I had the distinct honor of working in Latin America as a Foreign Service Officer in the Department of State.

By crossing sectors – from public to private to non-profit – I have seen the impact that U.S. engagement in the Western Hemisphere can have. I'd like to focus today specifically on the economic importance of remaining engaged with our neighbors to the south. My comments today will draw largely from my experience in Mexico and South America as an IBMer working to promote scientific and computational collaboration with companies in the natural resources and finance sectors.

Very often, U.S. engagement with our neighbors to the south is predicated on some sort of crisis – avian flu, immigration, drug trafficking, etc. and its impact on us. All too often, we have overlooked the tremendous growth in Latin America and Brazil over the past decade. Simply paying lip service to the BRIC and the follow-on countries has done a disservice to the hard work that has been done collaboratively, the best practices that have been adopted from U.S. industry, and the international exchanges that have occurred. I like to say that the importance of Latin America is better summed up in a Spanish word than in an English word. In Spanish, the word "intercambio" sums up the benefits that accrue to all business parties in the relationships we develop in the Western Hemisphere. An "intercambio" is an interchange – kind of a clumsy word in English, but quite elegant in what it implies. We no longer "teach" or "train" our neighbors. We no longer "provide guidance" or improve their lots simply by providing our goods, services, or intellectual capital. The intercambios that exists today are multi-directional streets. Really, they are the super-highways of information and knowledge exchange. All parties involved benefit, and this leads to economic growth.

Economic Perspective on the Region: Defining U.S. Economic Interests in the Western Hemisphere

For decades, the U.S. corporate and trade focus on Latin American economies has been on lower value products: commodities, raw materials, etc. Any economist will say that these building blocks are critical to more developed markets in search of inputs for higher-valued manufactured and industrial products. And, of course, the outcome of this economic relationship always favors the market producing higher valued goods and services. Emerging market country strategies have, for years, focused on going "up the value chain" in terms of the values of their inputs. Some countries have hit the mark. South Korea is probably the most successful example of an "Asian Tiger" over the past two decades – moving from low margin inputs for technology and manufacturing industries and living in the shadow of Japan to being a world leader in technology and R&D, along with high end manufacturing. Several Latin American countries' economies have seen successes that mirror the Asian Tigers, although none has been as successful as South Korea.

Still in all, when U.S. companies are looking for countries in which to invest, countries where there are good prospects for growth, countries where the return on their investments, long-term, will be reasonable, countries where strong partnerships can be formed, it makes sense to look toward Latin America.

Why is the Western Hemisphere Important for U.S. Economic and Business Interests?

The global economy calls for diversification of investments – we know this as it relates to personal investments, and it is no less true for corporate investments. Successful countries where we used to have bilateral government-to-government relationships based on foreign assistance and dependency have morphed into countries where businesses can have relationships based on mutual interests and growth.

Colombia is an example of U.S. foreign assistance that worked. Plan Colombia provided Colombia's leaders in the late 90s and early 2000's with needed assistance to combat narcoterrorists. Under the leadership of President Uribe and his advisers in Bogota, some of whom were educated in the United States, Colombia successfully routed the majority of the narcoterrorists. President Santos has the relative luxury of being able to negotiate with the remaining FARC rebels from a position of strength in an attempt to end their continued violence and terror strikes on the nation and its infrastructure. Today, Colombia is a thriving democracy and an economic and financial powerhouse in the region. Additionally, many of the well-educated Colombians who fled their country (often finding safe haven in the United States) are now returning from diaspora. They are taking leading roles in Colombian industry and opening new enterprises in Colombia while also opening their doors to U.S. investors and partners. Medellin, once the drug capital of the world under the infamous Pablo Escobar, is now one of the leading financial and industrial centers in Latin America. Colombia's largest bank, Bancolombia (NYSE: CIB), is headquartered in Medellin and has revenues of nearly $6B with branches throughout Latin America and in the Untied States. This once profoundly dangerous city is now listed by Forbes Magazine as one of the 10 best cities in the world for international retirees.

Colombia is no longer a country looking for handouts or seeking international assistance with its problems. Colombia is now a "Latin Tigre." Another example of its success is in the oil industry. Colombia's oil giant, Ecopetrol (NYSE: EC), is a parastatal company that is half owned by the government and half publicly traded. Ecopetrol is regarded as a well-managed giant with revenues of nearly $38B. The current downturn in oil prices has certainly impacted Ecopetrol, but its asset base and reserves will allow it to weather the economic storm. Ecopetrol invests heavily not just in exploration and production – in Colombia and around the world (including the Gulf of Mexico). But it also invests heavily in R&D. It's scientific staff is based on a university-like campus in Bucaramanga and engages in deep scientific research using sophisticated super computers and advanced methodologies to develop in-house intellectual property. Many of their scientists received PhDs in the United States, and they have been returning to Bucaramanga both for quality of life improvements and in order to develop the Colombian petroleum industry as leading experts. I have worked personally with many of them, and I can attest to the quality of their work. It is published and presented, in Engish and in Spanish – it is world-class.

Colombia lets the world know that it is "open for business." Indeed, in 2014, it rose from spot #53 to spot #34 on the World Bank's "Ease of Doing Business" index.

Brazil represents a country that is far enough away from the United States that it has not been as impacted by the United States as some of its neighbors – for good or for ill. It has largely grown and flourished on its own – the biggest player in its backyard.

Brazil's period of prosperity, when the BRIC was the preeminent force of nature in emerging markets (around the turn of the 21st century), began in the late 1990s with decisions made by the government of Fernando Cardoso to denationalize some of Brazil's government-owned enterprises (steel milling, telecommunications, and mining). Moving massive and poorly performing industries into private industry allowed for sustained growth of around 5%/year.

The privatization push in Brazil continued, and industries have thrived. Brazil's natural resources (oil/gas, minerals/mining, agriculture), manufacturing (aircraft, automobiles, steel), financial, IT, and healthcare/life sciences sectors have all thrived and grown over the years. However, the Brazilian government, beginning under Luiz Ignacio "Lula" da Silva and continuing under President Dilma Roussef, has often looked at the economic miracle of Brazil as a means to provide expanded and (sometimes) unaffordable services to the country's large population.

The result of expanded social services is a strained education system with sometimes mismatched resources (e.g., there are not enough petroleum engineers being trained and perhaps too many social scientists). Other strains are seen in a heavy tax burden, one of the highest in the world on personal income, sales tax, and corporate revenues/profits. Brazil, once the darling of the BRIC, has become a burdensome place and is near the bottom of the list of the World Bank's "Ease of Doing Business" index, in the unenviable 120th place.

Brazil, under President Dilma Roussef, has been wracked by charges of corruption around the country's parastatal oil/gas behemoth, Petrobras (NYSE: PBR). Indeed, corruption allegations marred her reelection campaign and, after her election victory, she promised to investigate corruption allegations. She has taken steps as well to shore up her economic team with advisers from the "University of Chicago School of Thought," including her newly-appointed Finance Minister Joachim Levy. Dilma certainly hopes these moves will help to move Brazil out of recession, where it has been floundering for the past several quarters, and where it is forecast to be for the next few, at least. Decreased economic growth is not what Dilma wants as her legacy, nor would this be of benefit to us in the United States.

The oil/gas industry, and Petrobras in particular, is the largest industry in Brazil. The U.S. and international companies have large-scale presences in Brazil, and they work in collaboration with Petrobras. It is in Brazil's interest to root out corruption in Petrobras in order to reassure global investors that their investments will be secure there. Allegations are that the corruption stems from the top.

International investors, including Americans, will not flee from Brazil. Brazil has the largest offshore oil discovery on earth. The offshore exploration and production off the coast of Rio de Janeiro will continue and expand for decades to come. The oil discoveries in Brazil will create jobs for Americans as well as Brazilians. Trained petroleum engineers, welders, mechanics, rig operators, drillers, safety officers, etc. will all be required for long term projects. Many of these people could be Americans with years of experience gained both in U.S. and foreign oilfields. Additionally, U.S. investments in operations in Brazil should reap rewards in the form of financial returns on their investments, should production continue over the years.

Of course the drop in oil prices worldwide has had an impact on the Brazilian economy, much as it has ours. But just as our oil and gas operations have not ground to a halt, neither have those in Brazil. While quarterly reports will, for the short term, remain flat or even lower (in Brazil's case, Petrobras's share price was down 30% just in the month of December), no one predicts the drop in oil prices, or demand for oil, to decline long term. Petrobras's financial outlook and debts may require it to restructure some of its finances in the short term, but long term prospects remain good.

What does Brazil's oil market have to do with jobs in the United States? As I just noted, on the one hand, Americans are being employed in significant numbers as expatriate subject matter experts in Brazil. On the other hand, expanded reserves in Brazil, with opportunities for U.S. investment by large U.S. oil companies means that U.S. oil companies have a geographic diversification of their holdings and can weather financial storms with less risk. This mitigated risk allows those same American companies to expand operations and employment very directly in the U.S. and in other operations abroad. U.S. equipment manufacturers can generate significant sales, in turn boosting our own economy and stimulating job creation at home. It means the continued growth of a critical American industry.

Brazil is not just oil-rich. Brazil is rich in all natural resources: Oil/gas, minerals, precious metals, farmland, water, livestock. Conceivably, Brazil could cut itself off from the rest of the world and survive on its own. Survive, but not necessarily thrive or grow. Brazil's natural resource wealth and its ability to move "up the value chain" from being a commodity supplier to being an integrator and manufacturer of finished goods has allowed Brail to cover a full range of export options. Brazil exports everything from soy to finished airplanes.

Who is buying Brazil's goods? Brazil's largest trading partner used to be the United States, but it is now commodities-hungry China. Behind the two largest trading partners is Brazil's third largest export market, Argentina.

I'd like to explore briefly the situation in **Argentina**. Like its neighbor Brazil, Argentina is rich in natural resources. It has everything from oil/gas to minerals to agriculture to vineyards and on and on. However, unlike Brazil, we all know that Argentina has squandered both international good will and patience. Argentina's government is so corrupt that its financial accounting is no longer accepted internationally. There is such limited transparency into things like its foreign reserve holdings and government spending and price-fixing that its inflation rate – spiraling upwards on a daily basis – is no longer even reported. The leadership of Kristina Fernandez de Kirchner is so corrupt that it now appears that, in cahoots with Iran, Kirchner may be behind the assassination of a Special Prosectuor, Alberto Nisman, the day he was to testify about his findings around the Amia Center bombing in 1994 in which 85 members of the Jewish community were murdered.

Argentina is corrupt. The national oil company, YPF, nationalized Spanish oil company Repsol's holdings in Argentina – valued at over $10B. YPF "negotiated" a settlement in which Repsol is to be reimbursed an adjusted $5B for the seizure. Foreign reserves are at such a low level that companies are forbidden from taking dollars, euros, etc. out of Argentina. Indeed, foreign companies with a presence in Argentina have to reinvest all profits in their Argentine entity – they cannot repatriate profits to corporate headquarters outside the country.

Why would companies, American or otherwise, choose to remain in Argentina? The intellectual capital in the country is world-class. Argentine universities are first-rate, many graduates study abroad, including thousands in the United States, and they choose to return home because of a profound sense of nationalism and good quality of life. Companies know that there is an excellent and loyal workforce available to them – clamoring for good jobs at competitive wages. Companies are also well aware of cycles – business cycles and political cycles. The reign of Kristina Kirchner and the party of Juan Peron will eventually pass, and there will be a rethinking of Argentina's role in the international business world. If companies can sustain operations without running at a loss in Argentina, then it is wise to stay the course and wait out the storm. The potential benefits are quite large. That said, short term business and investment in Argentina is not for the fainthearted. The country occupies spot #124 on the World Bank's "Ease of Doing Business" index.

For many years, **Chile** held a role as the darling of Latin American business that is slowly being supplanted by Colombia. Chile remains a financial and mining industry giant in the region, but the newly-returned presidency of Michele Batchelet has many in industry seeing the return of more socialist tendencies that are less business-friendly. The new tax regime will be the first test of the global business community's patience with Chile.

There should be no misunderstanding here. No one is rushing for the doors in Chile – the business climate there remains robust and growing. The fact that Chile's economy, on some levels, remains highly dependent on the world's appetite (especially China's) for natural resources has been a source of some concern for companies. But the fact that Chile is the world's number one producer of copper ensures that it will not be forsaken as market needs change. Yes, there may be some economic softening, but the bottom line is that Chile's economy is strong and is viewed as a strong, long-term continued economic player. Indeed, Chile's place on the World Bank's "Ease of Doing Business" index, slot #41, indicates its significance in the international marketplace.

Chile is also one of the most educated countries, per capita, in Latin America. Large numbers of Chilean students study in American colleges and universities each year and make use of their educations in their home country. This melding of American experiences with national capabilities further builds the international network that leads so many corporations to Chile. Adding to that network are the facts that Chile's banking and finance regulations are considered open and transparent, its unemployment rate is low (approx. 6% in 2013), and its labor force is diversified (across agriculture, industry, and services). The economic climate in Chile is excellent.

What does this mean for U.S. companies, exports, and jobs? High per capita income means that Chileans import more – their reasonable (for now) tax code indicates that this will continue. There are markets within Chile's middle class for American products. The diversified nature of the economy, with approximately 13% of the labor force engaged in agriculture, ensures that Chile's agriculture exports reach U.S. markets during "off-season." It used to be the case, at least when I was growing up, that you could only get certain fruits in the grocery store when they were "in season," and we all looked forward to the summer growing season. The winter in the U.S. is summer growing season in Chile, and we all, literally, reap the fruits of the Chilean harvests and exports during that time of the year.

It also means that there is a ready and open market for our exports. The seasons never end in this relationship.

A highly educated workforce in Chile also means that U.S. companies can work with Chileans – in the U.S. and/or in Chile. U.S. and Chilean mining companies operate extensively in Chile, cooperating and collaborating to extract minerals using best practices derived from each country's global experiences. American mining companies certainly learned lessons in 2010 when Chilean mining officials rescued 33 miners trapped in a collapsed mine in the remote Atacama region of the country. Indeed, the entire world learned lessons.

Chile's services industry is the largest part of its economy (64%). This is indicative of the advances in Chile's economy – from raw materials/commodity provider to world markets to services provider. The services are widely considered to be world-class, whether in outsourcing of back office operations or financial services or education and training. American companies maintain offices in Chile in order to ensure that they have a strong foothold in South America that is focused on delivery and growth.

An example of this is a Fortune 500 company, Air Products and Chemicals (NYSE: APD) based in Allentown, PA. Air Products acquired a 2/3 stake in Chilean company, Indura, in 2012 at a value of nearly $1B. The strategy behind the acquisition was to increase Air Products' sales of industrial gases and welding equipment in Latin America and to make Air Products the second biggest provider of industrial gases in Latin America, with $1.5B in annual sales. It was, at the time, Air Products' largest acquisition to date. When explaining the acquisition, then CEO John McGlade said that Indura would expand Air Products' geographic presence and add additional growth opportunities – it would balance Air Products' global portfolio. For Air Products, Latin America is the next-highest growth region in the world after Asia.

Why not start this discussion about the importance of the Western Hemisphere to U.S. business and trade with a discussion of **Mexico**? I believe that we all already know a lot about Mexico, and I wanted to introduce thinking about some of the critically important countries in South America that are driving growth in our half of the world. I also wanted to use Mexico and its role as leader among Spanish-speaking countries to drive growth worldwide. Mexico is the second largest economy in Latin America (behind Brazil), and it wields a tremendous amount of influence due in no small part to its proximity to the world's economic golden goose – us.

We can discuss the importance of Mexico's significance to the U.S. economy and job creation for days or months or years. But the realization of Mexico's criticality was made evident through NAFTA 20 years ago and has only grown. Mexico currently sits at spot #39 on the World Bank's "Ease of Doing Business" index.

After the U.S. and Canada, Mexico is the third-largest oil producer in the Western Hemisphere and the 10th largest in the world, but its hydrocarbons industry has been in decline. The 75-year old state monopoly known Pemex has crippled Mexican competitiveness in the sector. Pemex was struggling to reverse a decline in production – from 3.4M barrels/day in 2004 to 2.5M barrels/day in 2014. However, in August of 2014, in a key win for President Enrique Pena Nieto's reform drive, the Mexican Senate voted 78-26 for the package of bills to overhaul the sector and breathe new life into Latin America's second largest economy. This victory took many by surprise given that Pena Nieto's PRI party has been historically opposed to touching the issue, both because of the votes generated by unionized oil workers who owe their jobs to the state and because of the anachronistic "patrimony" grounds preventing U.S. and other foreign energy firms from entering the market.

Major U.S. and international oil companies have kept a close eye on the legislation. The Mexican government hopes the reform will bring needed technologies to Mexico to enhance exploration efforts both for oil and gas from hydraulic fracturing in shale formations and for oil in the deep water Gulf of Mexico. However, the legislation as it stands in early 2015 is overly complicated and needs further revisions. These modifications would require further streamlining of regulatory oversight and an even more diminished role for Pemex. The U.S. Government can assist Mexico by facilitating trade, regulatory reform, and infrastructure development, all of which will benefit both countries. The U.S. should continue to encourage additional market-oriented reforms.

Part of the August overhaul will reduce Pemex's tax burden – a burden so great that, over the past ten years, Pemex only twice cleared a small profit after its state contributions. This has undermined Pemex's ability to invest in research, technology, and human capital. It has also been subject to budgetary oversight– the lack of autonomy has kept it from being competitive. One of the most controversial measures in the recently passed legislation calls for the government to absorb part of the Pemex workers union's unfunded pension liabilities, currently over $125B – equal to 10% of Mexico's GDP. Workers would then have to renegotiate their labor contract with Pemex.

Mexico must attract private companies for its energy sector to recover and grow. The reform legislation will allow private companies to sign profit-sharing contracts as soon as 2015 to drill for oil and natural gas. Industry giants will not invest in Mexico if the regulatory environment is unfavorable or uncertain, but also if it is uncompetitive.

Mexico is on the cusp of a significant boom in jobs related to the oil and gas industry, but it also faces a short-term human capital crunch. If private and foreign companies begin operations in Mexico, the 160 petroleum engineers graduating each year from Mexican universities will fall far short of demand. On the regulatory side, it is estimated that the National Hydrocarbon Commission alone will require 500-600 specialized staff to regulate the sector. It currently employs 51. The Mexican government should promote exchanges between national and international universities, companies, and think tanks to promote human capital development in Mexico.

Of course there are questions of security that present challenges to Mexico's long-term energy success. Many of the most promising shale prospects are in the northeast, which coincides with many hot spots of drug-related violence. This could stave off some foreign investment, but most international energy firms are used to operating in hostile environments. Their decisions about Mexican operations will be driven by projections of security costs vs. potential revenue.

Mexico is the lynchpin country in forming the **Pacific Alliance**, a free trade area comprised of Mexico, Colombia, Peru, and Chile. It was formed as a counterbalance to the Mercosur trade bloc (Brazil, Argentina, Venezuela, Uruguay, and Paraguay). The counterweight, though, packs quite a punch. In its first year, the Pacific Alliance's trade with external partners outpaced Mercosur's. The pattern appears likely to continue. State control in the largest Mercosur countries will be a continued limiting factor on U.S. investments in the region.

This newly-formed trade bloc of Latin American "Tigres" shows great promise in the global economy. The IMF notes that last year, Mercosur member countries had average growth of 0.6%, while Pacific Alliance countries had average growth of 4.2%. Indeed, Pacific Alliance countries are attracting foreign direct investment that would otherwise have been directed toward Brazil, Argentina, and Venezuela.

We should not relax, however, and think that U.S. companies can sit back and reap the rewards from relationships that are driven by geography. The name of the emerging trade bloc gives clues as to its orientation. A pivot to Asia.

Latin countries have seen how an American sneeze can cause a regional cold. They have learned the importance of diversification. This is true not just as it relates to their export capabilities, but regarding their export markets as well. Chile has vastly expanded exports in agriculture, fish/seafood, wines, minerals, financial products, and services. Colombia has moved beyond raw materials and into finished goods, services, minerals, oil and gas, and of course coffee and flowers. Peru is branching beyond its traditional exports. And Mexico can export almost anything we can export.

The Pacific Alliance Tigres are eyeing Asia. Not just China, but other Asian markets as well. This will make Alliance members more competitive globally, and it will mitigate some of the risk that might come from an American sneeze.

Indeed, the super highway I referenced earlier is every bit a present-day reality. American businesses must fasten their seatbelts for the ride along it. Businesses should remain engaged so as not to lose market share to China and the Asian Tigers. Engagement, investment, collaboration, partnership, and active participation all ensure that our businesses will grow, we will continue to hold a footprint in the most stable region outside North America, and we will create jobs and investment opportunities for Americans at home and abroad.

Mr. DUNCAN. Thank you.

I am going to ask the witnesses try and stay on time, if you can. Dr. Ellis, you are recognized for 5 minutes. Thank you.

STATEMENT OF EVAN ELLIS, PH.D., AUTHOR

Mr. ELLIS. Thank you. Chairman Duncan, Ranking Member Sires, distinguished committee members, thank you for the opportunity to share my analysis with you today. I will summarize my written remarks for the committee.

I wish to highlight the four challenges in Latin America and the Caribbean—organized crime, Russia, Islamic radicalism, and China.

The passage of drugs, immigrants, and illicit goods through the region to the United States continues to fuel criminal organizations, deepening the crisis violence and the lack of opportunity in those societies.

El Salvador's facilitation of a truce between Mara Salvatrucha and Barrio 18 in 2012 and the Guatemalan President Otto Perez Molina's appeal to legalize drugs to reduce the violence and criminality in his country shows just how desperate the situation has become.

Trans-Pacific crime also merits more attention. Recent examples include the sourcing of precursor chemicals by the Sinaloa cartel from Chinese mafias, metal ore shipments to China from cartel-controlled parts of Michoacan and the use of Chinese banks to launder money by the Brazilian gang First Capital Command.

Russia—Russia is the external actor which has most openly challenged the United States in Latin America. Since 2008, it has repeatedly deployed military aircraft, warships, and submarines close to the United States including three port calls in Havana by the signals intelligence ship Viktor Leonov most recently on January 20th, the day before our U.S. Government team headed toward Havana to meet with Cuban officials.

Russia's defense minister, Sergei Shoigu, said last February that his country seeks to resupply and maintain its warships in Nicaragua, Cuba, and Venezuela; to operate its military aircraft from their airfields, and possibly to reopen the Cold War era surveillance facility at Lourdes, Cuba.

Last November, Minister Shoigu further said that Russia would send long-range bombers to fly patrols near the U.S. including in the Caribbean and the Gulf of Mexico.

Iran—Iran has used Embassy personnel to recruit terrorists in the region including those by Mohsen Rabbani, who developed networks of operatives throughout region such as the Guyanese emir and Islamic radical Abdul Kadir sentenced in 2010 for the plot to attack the JFK Airport.

Latin America is also a source of terrorist financing including the narco trafficker Chekry Harb and the money launderer Ayman Joumaa, who channeled part of their drug earnings to Hezbollah and other terrorist organizations.

Terrorists also conduct operations in the region. Just 3 months ago, for example, Hezbollah operative Muamad Amadar was arrested near Lima, Peru, stockpiling explosives for use in that country.

The recent suspicious death of Argentine special prosecutor, Alberto Nisman, the day before his testimony to the Argentine Congress does raise disturbing questions about the current Argentine Government's relationship with Iran.

China—the PRC has most significantly impacted the region's security environment although not openly challenging the United States. Of the more than $100 billion it has loaned to the region since 2005, three-quarters of that have gone to the ALBA regimes in Argentina, helping to keep governments like Venezuela's solvent so that they could continue to operate as bases for criminals and as entry points for other actors who would do us harm.

China has also chosen CELAC, which excludes the United States and Canada, rather than the Organization of American States as its preferred vehicle for building its relationships with the region.

The PRC has expanded its military activities in Latin America, undermining U.S. efforts to remain the security partner of choice. In October 2013, while Washington was distracted by the budget crisis, a PLA naval flotilla for the first time conducted combat exercises with our allies in Chile as well as with Brazil.

Chinese companies sell military aircraft, helicopters, satellites, trucks and armored vehicles to both U.S. partners and its adversaries in the region and possibly sales to Argentina of the FC–1 fighter, the P–18 Corvette, the X–11 helicopter and the V–1 armored personnel carrier.

My recommendations—there is a need to think more strategically about the contribution of Latin America and the Caribbean to U.S. national security and prosperity; to see it as more than simply a source of drugs and immigrants that needs to be controlled.

The U.S. rapprochement with Cuba and the April Summit of the Americas provide an opportunity to reinvigorate the OAS as the premier multilateral institution for the Americas. The U.S. can also facilitate engagements by other actors whose priorities are consistent with our objectives in the region including India, Japan, and South Korea.

I also recommend greater attention to how in a major conflict involving the United States elsewhere in the world our adversaries might use their commercial position and assets in the region to shape the outcome by impacting U.S. coalition formation, deployments, sustainment, and political will.

Finally, we need to be clear to ourselves where we draw the line regarding activities by extra hemisphere actors in the region that potentially threaten our national security and, further, to make those lines known to them in less ambiguous terms than has occurred to date.

Thank you, Mr. Chairman.

[The prepared statement of Mr. Ellis follows:]

R. Evan Ellis, Ph.D
Research Professor of Latin American Studies
Carlisle Barracks, PA

Testimony to the Subcommittee on the Western Hemisphere
Foreign Affairs Committee
U.S. House of Representatives
Tuesday, February 3, 2015

**"The Strategic Importance of the Western Hemisphere:
Defining U.S. Interests in the Region"**

Chairman Duncan, ranking member Sires, distinguished committee members, thank you for the opportunity to share my analysis with you today. While I am a Research Professor at the U.S. Army War College Strategic Studies Institute, I am here today in my personal capacity and, as such, these views are my own and do not represent the position of the Army War College, the US Army, or the Department of Defense.

There is arguably no region more critical to the security and prosperity of the United States than Latin America and the Caribbean. The U.S. trades with and invests more in the region than with any other part of the world, binding our well-being to that of Latin America and the Caribbean.

The 17% of U.S. residents of Hispanic origin also highlights how we are connected to the region by bonds of family.

Through our shared land and maritime borders, the ills that occur in the region are transmitted to this country in the form of refugees, criminal activities, and openings for terrorists and state rivals, who would use it as a base from which to do us harm.

Today, I wish to highlight four interrelated challenges in Latin America and the Caribbean, which I respectfully submit merit this Subcommittee's attention: organized crime, Russia, Islamic radicalism, and China.

Organized crime. In Mexico and Central America, the passage of drugs and immigrants toward the United States continues to fuel transnational criminal organizations, street gangs, and other illicit groups, deepening the crisis of violence, corruption, impunity and lack of opportunity in parts of those societies—particularly in El Salvador, Honduras and Guatemala. Such conditions, in turn, also create spaces in which actors disposed to harm the United States may operate.

In Mexico, just two weeks ago, David Arellano Cuan, head of legal affairs in the country's Interior Ministry, warned that 75% of Mexico's municipalities are vulnerable to infiltration by organized crime.[1] At that same hearing, the head of criminal investigations in the Mexico's Attorney Generals' office, Tomas Zeron de Lucio, called the level of municipal police corruption in the country "alarming."[2]

Mexico's government reports that it has captured or killed more than 80 of the nation's 122 most wanted criminals.[3] Yet with more than 80,000 Mexican lives lost since 2006 in the conflict, it is not clear whether the situation has improved.

I also worry that momentum has been lost in the historic expansion of mutual respect and confidence that occurred between our governments and armed forces since 2006. In addition, according to 2013 data, extraditions of criminals to the United States under President Peña Nieto are proceeding at a rate of less than half of what they were under his predecessor.[4]

In Central America, the surge in immigrant children arriving at the U.S. border last spring, the willingness of El Salvador government, to broker a truce (which has now collapsed) between the rival street gangs Mara Salvatrucha and Barrio 18,[5] and the September 2012 appeal by conservative Guatemalan President Otto Perez Molina that violence and criminality is so out of control that the region should consider legalizing drugs,[6] shows just how desperate the situation has become.

One illustrative case is Honduras. Like others in the region, it was designated by the White House in 2014 as a "major drug transit and/or major illicit drug producing country." Its president, Juan Orlando Hernandez, has publicly declared that the transnational criminal organizations operating there are as aggressive and cause as much destruction as Middle Eastern terrorist groups like ISIL.[7] Indeed, in 2013, Honduras had the highest murder rate in the world, at 79 per 100,000, while only one percent of such homicides in major cities result in convictions of the perpetrator.[8]

In the Caribbean, the flow of cocaine has reached levels not seen for more than a decade, with 91 metric tons seized in 2013.[9]

The situation is compounded by both the external and domestic policies of the ALBA regimes, where high levels of public corruption combine with an unwillingness to cooperate with Western law enforcement to effectively creates sanctuaries for transnational criminal organizations operating in the region. In 2014, pursuant to section 706(1) of the Foreign Relations Authorization Act of 2003 (Public Law 107-228), the administration designated the ALBA regimes Venezuela and Bolivia as not complying with their international obligations in the fight against narcotics.[10] Last week, Venezuelan security official and presidential bodyguard Leamsy Salizar fled to the United States, collaborating with U.S. authorities and publicly naming Diosdado Cabello, his former boss and President of Venezuela's National Assembly, as the head of the "Cartel of the Suns," Venezuela's principal transnational criminal organization.[11]

In addition, the still modest but growing threat of trans-pacific crime involving the region also merits more attention. Dimensions of concern include human smuggling, precursor chemicals, illegal mining, other contraband goods, and money laundering.[12]

Illustrative of such problems, a major operation by the Mexican Navy in the state of Michoacán in November 2013 exposed a transpacific criminal production chain in which ore illegally mined in territory under the control of the Knights Templar criminal organization was bought by criminal middlemen and eventually shipped to the PRC.[13] Similarly, the February 2014 takedown of Sinaloa Cartel boss "El Chapo" Guzman led to the public exposure of his organization's ties across the Pacific, including operations the Philippines, and precursor chemicals sourced from Chinese mafia organizations such as Sun Yee On and Sap Sze Wui [14] In Brazil, a recent government investigation found that the transnational criminal organization First Capital Command (PCC), one of the largest such groups in the country. is using bank accounts in the PRC, as well as in the United States, to launder money.[15]

Russia. Of the external actors with an interest in the region, Russia is the one which has most openly challenged the United States. Since 2008, Russia has repeatedly deployed nuclear-capable aircraft, warships, and submarines within close proximity to this country. In November 2013, a Tu-160 bomber violated the airspace of U.S. ally Colombia in a transit between Nicaragua and Cuba.[16] In addition, signals intelligence ship Viktor Leonov has been operating in the Caribbean, making at least three port calls in Havana Harbor in the past year, including in February and March 2014 as tensions between the US and Russia heated up over Ukraine,[17] and most recently, on January 20th of this year, as Assistant Secretary of State for the Western Hemisphere Roberta Jacobson and her team headed to Havana to advance the normalization of relations between our government and Cuba. [8]

Since 2001, Russia has sold Latin America $14.5 billion in arms, of which approximately $11 billion has gone to Venezuela, [9] although Brazil, Peru, and Nicaragua have also been important customers.[20] Moscow is also working with Nicaragua in counterdrug operations,[21] and has established a regional training center in Managua, giving Russian instructors the opportunity to interact with visiting security personnel from across the region.[22]

Russia has also signaled its intent to expand its military presence in the region. In February 2014, its Defense Minister Sergei Shoigu expressed his government's intent to pursue agreements with Nicaragua, Cuba and Venezuela to allow Russian military ships and aircraft to resupply in the ports and airports of those countries, as well as possibly re-opening the large Cold War era surveillance facility in Lourdes, Cuba.[23]

Las November, Minister Shoigu added to such declarations of intent, announcing Russian plans to send bombers and other Russian military aircraft on long range patrols in proximity to the U.S. coast, including flights into the Caribbean and Gulf of Mexico.[24]

Islamic Radicalism. Iran's current president Hassan Rouhani, in contrast to his predecessor Mahmoud Ahmadinejad, has not publicly pursued alliances with anti-US leaders in Latin America and the Caribbean. Yet Iran has used its embassy personnel to recruit and radicalize would be terrorists in the region, who have then planned operations against the United States. Examples of such Iranian officials include former cultural attaché to Argentina Mohsen Rabbani, implicated in the 1994 attack against the AMIA Jewish cultural center in Argentina, and believed to have been one of Iran's lead recruiters of Islamic radicals in the region. One of the people whom he is believed to have recruited is Abdul Kadir, a Guyanese convert to Islamic radicalism, sentenced to life in prison in 2010 for a plot to detonate bombs under New York's JFK airport.[25]

The death of Argentine Special Prosecutor Alberto Nisman by a gunshot to the head, the day before he was to testify to the Argentine Congress regarding an alleged cover-up of Iran's role in the 1994 AMIA attack by Argentine President Cristina Fernandez de Kirchner and her government, raises disturbing questions regarding that government's relationship with Iran and Islamic radicals.

While it is not clear to what degree Iranian activities in Latin America have continued under President Rouhani, Latin America continues to be a source of terrorist financing, including a portion of the otherwise legitimate remittances and charitable donations sent from Islamic businessmen in the region, as well as illicit activities such as those by the narcotrafficker Chekry Harb, and by Ayman Joumaa, who laundered money for Los

Zetas; both men channeled a portion of their earnings to the terrorist organization Hezbollah.[26]

Latin America and the Caribbean also continues to provide fertile ground for terrorist recruitment, including the previously mentioned JFK Airport plot by Guyanese nationals Abdul Kadir and Abdel Nurwere, and more recently, Muamad Amadar, arrested near Lima, Peru in October 2014, believed to be a Hezbollah operative stockpiling explosives in his apartment for use against targets in the country.[27]

PRC. China, in its pursuit of economic objectives in Latin America and the Caribbean also has impacted the region's security environment. Of the more than $100 billion that its banks have loaned to the region since 2005, more than ¾ has gone to the nations of ALBA and Argentina,[28] including more than $9 billion lent to the regime of Nicholas Maduro in Venezuela since the death of his predecessor Hugo Chavez in March 2013. The PRC has also committed almost $20 billion to Ecuador, including $7.5 billion in new credit, just announced during President Correa's January 2015 visit to Beijing.[29]

While the PRC has been cautious not to associate itself with the anti-US rhetoric and activities of the ALBA regimes, its money has sustained their viability, enabling countries such as Venezuela to continue as de facto sanctuaries for criminal and insurgent groups, and also, as points of entry into the region for Russia, Iran and other actors with potentially hostile intentions toward the United States.

Chinese resources also contribute to ALBA efforts to undercut the region's established institutions for multilateral democratic interaction, including the Organization of American States. In recent years, ALBA regimes have created obstacles to the use of the OAS to address important regional issues, and have withdrawn their personnel from OAS institutions such as the Interamerican Defense College, while simultaneously attempting to create substitute institutions that explicitly exclude the U.S. and Canada, such as UNASUR and the Community of Latin American and Caribbean States

(CELAC), and to use such substitute institutions to address the region's most important issues.

Indeed, the PRC has directly contributed to the promotion of institutions that exclude the U.S., rather than working through the OAS and established Interamerican system. Although the PRC has been welcomed as an observer at the OAS since 2004, it has chosen CELAC, which explicitly excludes the United States and Canada, as its preferred vehicle for engaging with Latin America and the Caribbean.[30]

The PRC has also expanded its military activities with Latin American and the Caribbean states. Institutional visits to the region by the People's Liberation Army, education and training for its officers in China, and gifts and sales of military material by Chinese companies are undermining U.S. efforts to remain the security partner of choice for Latin American and Caribbean countries.[31]

Chinese military companies such as the NORINCO group are also now selling radars, fighter aircraft, military helicopters, trucks and armored vehicles to Venezuela, Bolivia and Ecuador.

Beyond the ALBA countries, Chinese arms companies have sold the Peruvian armed forces Beiben, Dong Feng, and Shaanxy military trucks, and have pursued contracts to supply 40 Type 90B multiple launch rocket vehicles to the country.[32] Chinese companies have also recently advanced into the sale of naval vessels to the region, agreeing last year to providing a patrol boat for Trinidad and Tobago,[33] and negotiating similar sales with Uruguay and Argentina.[34] The PRC is also in negotiations to sell its FC-1 fighter to Argentina, just as Russia is trying to sell Argentina its Su-24 bomber,[35] either of which would create a threat to the British position in the Falkland Islands.[36]

PLA military activities in Latin America and the Caribbean have expanded from multilateral humanitarian exercises, such as participation in the MINUSTAH peacekeeping operation in Haiti from 2004 through 2012, to bilateral activities such as a November 2010 disaster response exercise with the Peruvian military, followed in 2011 by deployment of the new PLA Navy hospital ship "Peace Arc" to conduct medical activities in the Caribbean.[37]

Moving beyond such humanitarian activities, in October 2013, while Washington was distracted by the federal budget crisis, a PLA naval flotilla crossed the Pacific, where, for the first time, Chinese warships conducted bilateral combat exercises with their counterparts in Chile[38] and Brazil,[39] as well as making a port call in Argentina.

While the PRC does not currently show an interest in establishing military bases or alliances in Latin America or the Caribbean, its expanding economic presence and commercial capabilities in the region in areas such as logistics, telecommunications, and space gives it numerous options for shaping the outcome of a crisis involving the US and our allies in Asia, were one to occur.[40]

I am concerned that, while public discussions of security challenges to the United States in the hemisphere correctly focus on issues such as drugs, organized crime and terrorism, they seldom include the equally important consideration of how, in the undesirable event of a major conflict involving the U.S. elsewhere in the world, our adversaries could use their commercial position and assets to impact U.S. coalition formation, deployment, sustainment, and political will.[41]

Despite such difficulties, there is arguably no other region in the world where the U.S. has as much of a comparative advantage for building strong partnerships and making a difference, than it does in Latin America and the Caribbean. What is needed, however, is more strategic thinking about the region, its connection to the world, and its contribution to U.S. security, prosperity, and the U.S. global posture broadly.

The U.S. should take advantage of the extraordinary opportunity provided by both reapproachment with Cuba and the upcoming summit of the Americas to reinvigorate the OAS as the primer multilateral institution for the Western Hemisphere, while opposing attempts through the empowerment of alternative organizations such as UNASUR and CELAC to exclude the U.S. from the region.[42]

For Mexico and Central America, we must show our partners that we are as focused on reducing narcotics demand in the U.S. and the flow of firearms to the region, as we are to stopping drug transits and dismantling criminal organizations in the region itself. From this base of confidence and trust, we can then work more effectively with those partners in pursuit of internationally coordinated, whole-of-government solutions, helping them strengthen their own institutions (as well as ours) to collectively become more secure and more prosperous.

The United States can also make it clearer to extra-hemispheric actors such as Russia, the PRC, and Iran where it draws the line between engagement in Latin America and the Caribbean, and actions which unacceptably undermine US security and other interests in the region.

Reciprocally, the U.S. can also do more to *facilitate* engagements by those extra-hemispheric actors whose objectives and practices are consistent with democracy, free markets, and the rule of law in the region, such as India, Japan, and South Korea. If our current era is the "Century of the Pacific," then one cornerstone of our strategy should be to coordinate with like-minded states on both the Asian and American sides of that ocean to advance projects such as the Trans-Pacific Partnership, and initiatives of others such as the Pacific Alliance, to ensure that the regime that prevails across the Pacific is one in which democratic states, respecting human rights, free markets, and the rule of law, can thrive.

There are also still other ways in this time of tight budgets that, without expensive new programs, the Administration and this Congress can demonstrate that Latin America and the Caribbean are fundamental for US security and prosperity. It would be refreshing, for example, for the President and Congressional leaders to mention the region more often when on trips to other parts of the world, just as visits to Latin America by Administration officials are filled with discussions of ISIL, Ebola, or North Korea.

Latin America and the Caribbean will also be listening, I suspect, for how many times the region is mentioned (other than for matters of immigration and border security), by candidates for the U.S. Presidency in 2016.

Arguably in no other part of the world does a region's prosperity and good governance so affect the well-being of the United States, and in no other region do failures so immediately bring economic refugees, criminal actors, and potentially, terrorists to our borders, as Latin America and the Caribbean.

For no other region is what happens there a matter of "family" as this region is for so many Americans. Latin America and the Caribbean deserve our attention; its security and prosperity are in our common interest.

---

[1] "75% de municipios tienen infiltración del crimen organizado: Segob," *Crónica*, January 21, 2015, http://www.cronica.com.mx/notas/2015/879412.html. See also Arron Daugherty, "75% of Mexico Municipalities Susceptible to Organized Crime: Official," *Insight Crime*, January 23, 2015, http://www.insightcrime.org/news-briefs/75-of-mexico-municipalities-susceptible-to-organized-crime-official.

[2] "Crimen organizado mandaba en 13 municipios de Guerrero: PGR," *Animal Político*, January 21, 2015, http://www.animalpolitico.com/2015/01/crimen-organizado-mandaba-en-13-municipios-de-guerrero-pgr. See also Arron Daugherty, "75% of Mexico Municipalities Susceptible to Organized Crime: Official," *Insight Crime*, January 23, 2015, http://www.insightcrime.org/news-briefs/75-of-mexico-municipalities-susceptible-to-organized-crime-official.

[3] Leticia Pineda, "Mexico arrests Beltran Leyva cartel chief," *Yahoo! News*, October 2, 2014, http://news.yahoo.com/mexico-captures-most-wanted-drug-cartel-kingpin-015758497.html.

[4] In the first half of 2013, Mexico extradited 19 persons to the United States, compared to 579 extradited during the six years of the Calderon administration. See Luis Pablo Beauregard, "'El Chapo' Guzmán consigue frenar su extradición a EE UU," *El País*, January 27, 2015, http://internacional.elpais.com/internacional/2015/01/27/actualidad/1422318809_357796.html. See also Loren Riesenfeld, "'El Chapo' Gains Ground in Fight Against Extradition," *Insight Crime*, January 27, 2015, http://www.insightcrime.org/news-briefs/el-chapo-gains-ground-fight-against-extradition.

[5] See, for example, Marguerite Cawley, "MS13 Expanding After Truce Collapse in El Salvador?" *Insight Crime*, June 2, 2014, http://www.insightcrime.org/news-briefs/ms13-expanding-after-truce-collapse-in-el-salvador.

[6] "Otto Pérez apoya legalizar marihuana y amapola," *Prensa Libre*, March 4, 2014, http://www.prensalibre.com/noticias/politica/Perez-apoya-legalizar-marihuana-amapola_0_1113488655.html.

[7] Silvia Blanco, ""La guerra al narco es una guerra que no es nuestra'" *El País*, October 1, 2014, http://internacional.elpais.com/internacional/2014/10/01/actualidad/1412199282_18830 7.html.

[8] German H. Reyes R., "'La investigación criminal está en detrimento': Fiscal Especial de Delitos contra la Vida," *Revistazo*, December 9, 2014, http://www.revistazo.biz/web2/index.php/nacional/item/997-"la-investigación-criminal-está-en-detriment. See also Kyra Gurney, "Honduras Solves 1% of Homicide Cases: Report," *Insight Crime*, December 19, 2014, http://www.insightcrime.org/news-briefs/honduras-solves-1-of-homicide-cases.

[9] Elyssa Pachico, "US Releases New Plan for Caribbean Drug Trafficking," *Insight Crime*, January 26, 2015, http://www.insightcrime.com/news-analysis/us-releases-new-plan-for-caribbean-drug-trafficking.

[10] "Presidential Determination -- Major Drug Transit or Major Illicit Drug Producing Countries for Fiscal Year 2015." White House, Official Website, September 15, 2014, http://www.whitehouse.gov/the-press-office/2014/09/15/presidential-determination-major-drug-transit-or-major-illicit-drug-prod.

[11] Antonio Maria Delgado, "Identifican a Diosdado Cabello como jefe del Cartel de los Soles," *El Nuevo Herald*, January 27, 2015, http://www.elnuevoherald.com/noticias/mundo/america-latina/venezuela-es/article8206548.html.

[12] For a detailed overview of growing trans-Pacific crime ties, see R. Evan Ellis, "Chinese Organized Crime in Latin America," *Prism*, Vol. 4, No. 1, December 1, 2012, pp. 67-77.

[13] "Los Templarios controlaban exportación minera a China desde Lázaro Cárdenas," *La Vanguardia*, January 5, 2014, http://www.vanguardia.com.mx/lostemplarioscontrolabanexportacionmineraachinadesde lazarocardenas-1917212.html.

[14] Julieta Pelcastre, "'El Chapo' conspires with Chinese mafias to produce synthetic drugs in Latin America," *El Dialogo*, February 19, 2014, http://dialogo-americas.com/en_GB/articles/rmisa/features/regional_news/2014/02/19/sinaloa-alianza-china.

[15] Bruno Ribiero, "PCC envia dinheiro do tráfico para Estados Unidos e China," *O Estado de São Paulo*, January 15, 2015, http://sao-paulo.estadao.com.br/noticias/geral,pcc-envia-dinheiro-do-trafico-para-estados-unidos-e-china,1619985. See also Kyra Gurney, "Brazil's PCC, Mimicking the Country, Shifts Towards China," *Insight Crime*, January 19, 2015, http://www.insightcrime.org/news-briefs/brazil-pcc-gang-launder-money-in-china-united-states.

[16] "Colombia entregó nota de protesta a Rusia por violación de espacio aéreo," *El Espectador*, November 6, 2013, http://www.elespectador.com/noticias/elmundo/colombia-entrego-nota-de-protesta-rusia-violacion-de-es-articulo-456989.

[17] "La presencia de un buque espía ruso en La Habana ante el comienzo del deshielo provoca recelo," *ABC*, January 21, 2015, http://www.abc.es/internacional/20150121/abci-cuba-eeuu-intriga-presencia-buque-espia-ruso-201501202144.html. See also Michael Winter, "Russian Spy Ship Visits Havana," *USA Today*, February 28, 2014, http://www.usatoday.com/story/news/world/2014/02/27/russia-cuba-warship/5876249/.

[18] Fred Weir, "Russia sends clear message - and spy ship - on eve of US-Cuba talks," *Christian Science Monitor*, January 21, 2015, http://www.csmonitor.com/World/Europe/2015/0121/Russia-sends-clear-message-and-spy-ship-on-eve-of-US-Cuba-talks-video.

[19] "Russia Seeks New Arms Deals on Growing Latin American Market," *RIA Novosti*, May 18, 2013, http://en.ria.ru/world/20130518/181219365/Russia-Seeks-New-Arms-Deals-on-Growing-Latin-American-Market.html.

[20] In December 2013, for example, the Peruvian military signed a contract to acquire an additional 24 Mi-171 helicopters in a contract valued at $528 million, in support of increasing the mobility of its forces operating in the region. See "El ministro de Defensa de Perú revisa en Moscú con su homólogo ruso los avances del contrato para el suministro de 24 Mi-171Sh-P Hip H," *Defensa*, September 4, 2014, http://www.defensa.com/index.php?option=com_content&view=article&id=13173:el-ministro-de-defensa-de-peru-revisa-en-moscu-con-su-homologo-ruso-los-avances-del-contrato-para-el-suministro-de-24-mi-171sh-p-hip-h&catid=55:latinoamerica&Itemid=163.

[21] In 2014, Russian intelligence reportedly helped Nicaragua to decommission more than a ton of cocaine. "Rusia busca ampliar relaciones con Nicaragua," *Estrategia y Negocios*, January 24, 2015, http://www.estrategiaynegocios.net/lasclavesdeldia/785285-330/rusia-busca-ampliar-relaciones-con-nicaragua.

[22] "Russia to open police anti-drug training centre in Nicaragua," *Jane's Intelligence Weekly*, March 25, 2013, https://janes.ihs.com.

[23] "Russia with plans for military bases in Nicaragua, Cuba and Venezuela," *Mercopress*, February 17, 2014, http://en.mercopress.com/2014/02/27/russia-with-plans-for-military-bases-in-nicaragua-cuba-and-venezuela.

[24] Greg Botelho and Faith Karimi, "Russia flexes muscles with long-range bomber flights near U.S. shores," *CNN*, November 13, 2014, http://www.cnn.com/2014/11/13/world/europe/russia-bombers-plan/index.html.

[25] See G. Sulzburger, "2 men convicted in Kennedy Airport Plot," *New York Times*, August 3, 2010, p. A1.

[26] Jason Ryan, "Lebanese Drug Lord Charged in US: Links to Zetas and Hezbollah," *ABC News*, December 13, 2011, http://abcnews.go.com/blogs/politics/2011/12/lebanese-drug-lord-charged-in-us-links-to-zetas-and-hezbollah/.

[27] Cecelia Valenzuela, "Terrorismo sin fronteras," *El Comercio*, September 29, 2014, http://elcomercio.pe/opinion/columnistas/terrorismo-sin-fronteras-cecilia-valenzuela-noticia-1767395. See also "Presunto miembro de Hezbolá fue detenido en Surquillo," *El Comercio*, Lima, Peru, October 28, 2014, http://elcomercio.pe/lima/ciudad/presunto-terrorista-hezbola-fue-detenido-surquillo-noticia-1767375?ref=nota_lima&ft=mod_leatambien&e=titulo.

[28] "China-Latin America Finance Database," Interamerican Dialogue, accessed January 18, 2015, http://thedialogue.org/map_list.

[29] Ed Adamczyk, "China agrees to financing for Ecuador, Venezuela," *United Press International*, January 8, 2014, http://www.upi.com/Top_News/World-News/2015/01/08/China-agrees-to-financing-for-Ecuador-Venezuela/6751420741127/.

[30] See R. Evan Ellis, "Strategic Insights: The China-CELAC Summit: Opening a New Phase in China-Latin America-U.S. Relations?" U.S. Army War College Strategic Studies Institute, January 27, 2015, http://strategicstudiesinstitute.army.mil/index.cfm/articles/The-China-CELAC-Summit/2015/01/27.

[31] For a detailed account of such sales, see R. Evan Ellis, *The Strategic Dimension of China's Engagement with Latin America, Washington DC:* William J. Perry Center for Hemispheric Defense Studies, 2013, http://chds.dodlive.mil/files/2013/12/pub-PP-ellis.pdf. See also R. Evan Ellis, *China – Latin America Military Engagement*, Carlisle Barracks, PA: U.S. Army War College Strategic Studies Institute, August 2011, http://www.strategicstudiesinstitute.army.mil/pubs/display.cfm?pubID=1077.

[32] Perú selecciona el sistema táctico de lanzacohetes múltiples Norinco tipo 90B," *Infodefensa*, January 10, 2014, http://www.infodefensa.com/latam/2014/01/10/noticia-selecciona-sistema-tactico-lanzacohetes-multiples-norinco.html. See also "El Ejército de Perú adquiere sistemas de artillería chinos por 38 millones de dólares," *Defensa*,

December 27, 2013,
http://www.defensa.com/index.php?option=com_content&view=article&id=11143:el-
ejercito-de-peru-adquiere-sistemas-de-artilleria-chinos-por-38-millones-de-
dolares&catid=55:latinoamerica&Itemid=163.

[33] Ridzwan Rahmat, "Trinidad and Tobago to receive Chinese-supplied patrol vessel,"
IHS Janes 360, March 12, 2014, http://www.janes.com/article/35273/trinidad-and-
tobago-to-receive-chinese-supplied-patrol-vessel.

[34] "Argentina escolhe a China como parceira para seus OPV," *Poder Naval*, January 27,
2015, http://www.naval.com.br/blog/2015/01/27/argentina-escolhe-a-china-como-
parceira-para-seus-opv/.

[35] "En busca de nuevos acuerdos militares entre Rusia y Argentina," *Russia Beyond the
Headlines*, January 20, 2015, http://es.rbth.com/internacional/2015/01/20/en_busca-
de_nuevos_acuerdos_militares_entre_rusia_y_argentina_46603.html.

[36] Gareth Wood, "Argentina looking to buy Anti-Ship Strike Fighter from China," *Fighter
Jet News*, January 1, 2015, https://fighterjetnews.wordpress.com/2015/01/01/argentina-
looking-to-buy-chinese-fighters-and-anti-shipping-missiles/.

[37] Jeff Franks, "Chinese navy hospital ship visits Cuba, Caribbean," *Reuters*, October
22, 2011, http://in.reuters.com/article/2011/10/21/idINIndia-60058520111021.

[38] "Armadas de China y Chile Realizaron Ejercicios Navales," *Noticias FFAA Chile*.
October 16, 2013, http://noticiasffaachile.blogspot.com/2013/10/armadas-de-china-y-
chile-realizaron.html.

[22] "PLAN taskforce conducts joint maritime exercise with Brazilian Navy," *Ministry of
National Defense, Peoples Republic of China*, Official Website, October 28, 2013,
http://eng.mod.gov.cn/DefenseNews-2013-10/28/content_4472787.htm.

[40] For a more detailed discussion of such scenarios, see R. Evan Ellis, "The Strategic
Relevance of Latin America for the United States," U.S. Army War College Strategic
Studies Institute, December 8, 2014,
http://strategicstudiesinstitute.army.mil/index.cfm/articles/The-Strategic-Relevance-of-
Latin-America/2014/12/08.

[41] For a more detailed discussion of such possibilities, see R. Evan Ellis, "Strategic
Insights: The Strategic Relevance of Latin America for the United States," U.S. Army
War College Strategic Studies Institute, December 8, 2014,
http://strategicstudiesinstitute.army.mil/index.cfm/articles/The-Strategic-Relevance-of-
Latin-America/2014/12/08.

[42] See, for example, R. Evan Ellis, "Re-Engagement with Cuba: The Strategic Calculus,"
War on the Rocks, December 18, 201 http://warontherocks.com/2014/12/re-
engagement-with-cuba-the-strategic-calculus/.

Mr. DUNCAN. Thank you. And the Chair will recognize Mr. Farnsworth for 5 minutes.

STATEMENT OF MR. ERIC FARNSWORTH, VICE PRESIDENT, COUNCIL OF THE AMERICAS AND AMERICAS SOCIETY

Mr. FARNSWORTH. Thank you very much, Mr. Chairman. Good morning. Congratulations to you for your chairmanship.

Thank you, Mr. Salmon, for his previous leadership and let me also thank Mr. Sires for your continued interest in these issues. To Mr. Meeks, it is wonderful to have you back, sir. We are looking forward to working with all of you in a bipartisan manner.

Mr. Chairman and Mr. Ranking Member, I would submit to you today that strategic U.S. interests in the Western Hemisphere are as profound as our interests almost anywhere else on the globe.

The region is directly connected to our own day to day well-being from economic prosperity and growth to national and energy security and promotion of our most fundamental values.

Let us be clear eyed about this. Our most immediate neighbors have the greatest impact on our strategic interests. It is significant and consequential that we have a northern neighbor, Canada, which is both our top trade partner and top energy supplier and which is stalwart in working with us to address the toughest global challenges.

At the same time, North America, including Mexico, our second largest export market and also our third largest energy supplier, is becoming a fully integrated production platform with tightly knit supply chains and ever deepening commercial ties.

As China and other nations have emerged to challenge the preexisting global economic order, the ties that bind us within North America have created economic efficiencies, built competitiveness and directly contributed to the economic growth our citizens both desire and deserve.

The challenges that Mexico continues to face on the security side are also our concern because they undermine the rule of law, vacuum up resources and have the potential to spill over onto us. So it is therefore critically important that we get relations with our two most immediate neighbors right.

Beyond North America, it is profoundly in the self-interest of the United States to see a hemisphere where every nation is, in Vice President Biden's words, middle class, democratic, and secure.

These are precisely the characteristics that define our best, longest lasting, and most effective global partnerships, and it is also why we believe so strongly that trade and investment expansion in the Western Hemisphere is a strategic issue.

In the first instance, trade and investment supports our own economic strength and security, as the President noted during his State of the Union Address in January, and we heard a number of statistics from Congresswoman Ros-Lehtinen so I won't repeat that in terms of the importance of the Western Hemisphere to the U.S. economy.

At the same time, trade and investment also support efforts to build and strengthen middle classes abroad, breaking down traditionally restrictive patterns of economic organization and offering greater opportunities to grow and innovate, supported by the rule of law.

Formal trade agreements reinforce these activities while linking our economies closer together on a more permanent basis consistent with U.S. values We can do more and we should, and I have several specific ideas along these lines in my written testimony.

Nonetheless, while regional economic progress over the past decade is noteworthy, continued success is not guaranteed. The dramatic fall in oil prices is already straining regional economies and reducing the growth on which continued poverty reduction depends.

Hydrocarbons are plentiful across the Western Hemisphere and, Mr. Chairman, you made that point very eloquently already, directly supporting U.S. energy security but petroleum dependent nations like Venezuela and its client states in the Caribbean Basin, among others, are now in deep economic trouble, having squandered immense wealth generated during the past decade of high energy prices.

And there is perhaps nothing more motivating for dramatic, even radical, political change that fosters populism or potentially worse than fear and prospects for economic stagnation or retrenchment and one needs to look no further than the recent elections in Greece to prove that particular point.

It is therefore also in our strategic interest to promote broad based economic growth in Central America and the Caribbean, and there is a significant role here for Congress.

As we were starkly reminded by the summer—by the summer of 2014 crisis of unaccompanied minors on our southwestern border, most of whom came from Central America, families will take desperate measures when their livelihoods are at stake and their personal security and the rule of law cannot be guaranteed. These issues are interconnected, significantly exacerbated if not caused by the illegal drug trade and gang culture in a number of countries.

That is one reason why it is so important that we have full economic and security cooperation with both of the drug transit and drug producing nations including across the full range of cyber crime law enforcement and why it is so harmful when such cooperation breaks down, as we have seen with regard to Venezuela.

Beyond the pressing need to improve dramatically the personal security profile in parts of the region, however, the Western Hemisphere is, thankfully, a region largely at peace with only last vestiges of guerrilla conflict ongoing in Colombia.

With that nation actively involved in the peace process, which the United States has done so much to enable through our active policy and financial support for the Colombian people on a bipartisan basis, we must now begin to think in terms of supporting the peace once an agreement is struck.

And finally, Mr. Chairman and Mr. Ranking Member, if I could offer just a very brief word about Latin America and the Caribbean in the overall global environment.

No longer can we assume that we can engage solely on our own terms. We must increasingly contend for the region in the manner that we traditionally have not had to do.

China's growing presence and long-term commitment is change in the economic and political dynamic. At the same time, Brazil's rise has been universally and appropriately praised but with its interest in developing an increasing global profile, coupled with an increased capacity to realize greater ambitions, we must also recognize the Brazilian pursuit of its own foreign policy interests does not always coincide with our preferences.

That is okay. Competition is good in both politics and business. But it does mean that we have to engage meaningfully with the region on a sustained and creative basis, finding ways to promote our interests effectively by working closely in partnership with others wherever we can while recognizing the rapidly changing nature of hemispheric relations.

Thank you again for the opportunity to testify. I look forward to your questions.

[The prepared statement of Mr. Farnsworth follows:]

COUNCIL OF THE **Americas**

THE STRATEGIC IMPORTANCE OF THE WESTERN
HEMISPHERE: DEFINING U.S. INTERESTS IN THE REGION

HEARING BEFORE THE U.S. HOUSE OF REPRESENTATIVES
COMMITTEE ON FOREIGN AFFAIRS
SUBCOMMITTEE ON THE WESTERN HEMISPHERE
FEBRUARY 3, 2015

ERIC FARNSWORTH
VICE PRESIDENT
COUNCIL OF THE AMERICAS

*** As Prepared for Delivery ***

Good morning, Mr. Chairman, Mr. Ranking Member, and Members. It is a pleasure to join you and the other distinguished panelists for today's discussion on the strategic importance of the Western Hemisphere and U.S. interests in the region. Thank you for the opportunity to testify on such a timely and important topic as you launch your oversight activities in this new Congress.

May I first congratulate you, Mr. Chairman, on taking over the leadership of this Subcommittee, and also thank Mr. Salmon for his previous Chairmanship. May I also thank you, Mr. Sires, for your continued commitment to these issues as the Ranking Minority Member both in the previous Congress and going ahead. On behalf of the Council of the Americas, we are looking forward to working with you and the other members of this Subcommittee to promote U.S. national interests during this very intensive and fluid moment in hemispheric affairs.

Mr. Chairman, Mr. Ranking Member, I would submit to you that strategic U.S. interests in the Western Hemisphere are as profound as our interests almost anywhere else on the globe. The region is directly connected to our own day-to-day economic well-being and national security, from economic prosperity and growth to energy security, personal security, and the promotion of our most fundamental values.

North America

Let's be clear-eyed about this: our most immediate neighbors have the greatest impact on our strategic interests. It is significant and consequential that we have a northern neighbor, Canada, which is both our top trade partner and top energy supplier, and which is stalwart in working with us to address the toughest global challenges. At the same time, North America including Mexico—our second largest export market and also third largest energy supplier—is becoming a fully integrated production platform, with tightly-knit supply chains and ever-deepening commercial ties. As China and other nations have emerged to challenge the pre-existing global economic order, the ties that bind us within North America have had the effect of increasing the size of our own internal markets, thus creating economic efficiencies, building competitiveness, and directly contributing to the economic growth our citizens both desire and deserve. The challenges that Mexico continues to face on the security side are also our concern, because they undermine the rule of law, vacuum up resources, and have the potential to spill over onto us. It is therefore critically important that we get relations with our two most immediate neighbors right. In that regard, I would note the positive trilateral meeting of North American foreign ministers that took place over the weekend in Boston. We also look forward to the next meeting of North American leaders in Canada at some point later this year, and urge that it be used to advance concretely the trilateral agenda.

A Deeper Association with Growing Economies

Beyond North America, as Vice President Joe Biden first said during a speech to the Council of the Americas in 2013, and I concur, it is profoundly in the self-interest of the United States to see a hemisphere where every nation is "middle class, democratic, and secure."

Economies with strong and growing middle classes tend to be more stable economically and politically, and vested in working within the prevailing global order rather than undermining it. They have higher expectations of good governance, transparency, and anti-corruption, and demand effective property rights and the rule of law. They begin to demand better opportunities for themselves and their children, emphasizing education, healthcare, and job creation in the formal economy, while also developing a greater sensitivity to environmental issues and a responsibility for sustainable economic development. And, of course, they have growing purchasing power and the desire and ability to procure the products we design and sell. These are precisely the characteristics that define our best, longest-lasting, and most effective bilateral partnerships, and why the dramatic reduction in poverty across the region is of such importance to us here in the United States.

That is also why we believe so strongly that trade and investment expansion in the Western Hemisphere is a strategic issue. In the first instance, trade and investment supports our own economic strength and security, as the President noted during his State of the Union address in January. Almost one third of the entire U.S. economy is built on trade, while over 45 percent of overall goods exports went to Western Hemisphere nations in 2013, with 34 percent of our imports coming from there. At the same time, trade and investment also support efforts to build and strengthen middle classes abroad, breaking down traditionally restrictive patterns of economic organization and offering greater opportunities to grow and innovate supported by the rule of law. Formal trade agreements reinforce these activities, while linking our economies closer together on a more permanent basis consistent with U.S. values. We have seen these positive results over more than 20 years of North American integration under NAFTA, as well as free trade agreements with Central America and the Dominican Republic, Peru, and Chile, and, most recently, with Colombia and Panama. We can do more, and we should, including the prompt conclusion and passage of the Trans-Pacific Partnership which includes Canada, Mexico, Peru, and Chile; the rapid incorporation of Colombia and perhaps certain Central American nations into a completed TPP and also APEC; the incorporation of both Canada and Mexico into Trans-Atlantic Trade and Investment Partnership negotiations with Europe; active support for the Pacific Alliance which currently includes four of our free trade partners; consolidation of existing hemispheric trade agreements under one omnibus umbrella to the TPP or other high standard approach; and heightened efforts to engage Brazil and other MERCOSUR nations toward expanded, freer trade.

Energy Security and Growth

Nonetheless, while regional economic progress over the past decade is noteworthy, continued success is not guaranteed. The dramatic fall in oil prices is already straining regional economies and the growth on which continued poverty reduction depends. Hydrocarbons are plentiful across the Western Hemisphere, directly supporting the reliability and security of the U.S. energy supply. Our ability to meet our energy needs through regional trade and investment relationships is crucial, while a fall in prices helps the U.S. consumers who have been the drivers of economic recovery. But the impact also goes in the other direction. Petroleum-dependent nations like Venezuela and its client states in the Caribbean Basin are now in deep economic trouble, having squandered immense wealth generated during the past decade of high energy prices. We may see the situation deteriorate further before it improves. Other nations including Mexico, Argentina, Brazil, Colombia, and Ecuador, which have been anticipating continued high energy prices as an engine of growth, are also now facing a potential new reality. More broadly, nations that depend on the sale of primary commodities are often prone to booms and busts. This has significant political implications: the ability of nations to meet the growing expectations of their expanding middle classes is circumscribed when available resources are constrained. And there is perhaps nothing more motivating for dramatic, even radical political change that fosters populism—or potentially worse—than fear and prospects for economic stagnation or retrenchment. One needs look no further than the late January 2015 elections in Greece to reinforce the point. It is precisely this reason why it is in U.S. strategic interests to help build broad-based, inclusive, value-added regional economic growth.

Strengthening National and Personal Security

And it is also in our strategic interests to find ways to help Central America and the Caribbean develop economically, and there is a significant role here for Congress. The administration has just announced a $1 billion dollar assistance program for Central America for FY2016, which we hope will be actively and favorably considered. As we were starkly reminded by the summer 2014 crisis of unaccompanied minors on our Southwestern border, most who came from Central America, families will take desperate measures when their livelihoods are at stake and their personal security and the rule of law cannot be guaranteed. These issues are interconnected, significantly exacerbated if not caused by the illegal drug trade and gang culture in a number of countries. As increasing attention is being paid to help Central America address these issues, we are also seeing these same concerns infecting the Caribbean as well as the urban centers of South America. That's one reason why it is so important that we have full economic and security cooperation with both the drug transit and drug producing nations, including across the full range of cybercrime law enforcement, and why it is so harmful when such cooperation breaks down. A more comprehensive approach to development is required.

Beyond the pressing need to improve dramatically the personal security profile in parts of the region, however, the Western Hemisphere is, thankfully, a region largely at peace, with only the last vestiges of guerrilla conflict ongoing in Colombia. With that nation actively involved in a peace process, which the United States has done so much to enable through our active policy and financial support for the Colombian people on a bi-partisan basis, we must now begin to think in terms of supporting the peace, once an agreement is struck. This will not be easy or inexpensive, but Colombia has proven itself through the years to be a reliable partner for the United States in South America, and in my view it will be equally important to offer tangible support for the implementation of potential peace accords in order to support our own strategic hemispheric goals.

A Changing Americas

Finally, Mr. Chairman and Mr. Ranking Member, let me offer a word about Latin America and the Caribbean in the overall global environment. In short, the region is in play. No longer can we assume that we can engage solely on our own terms. We must increasingly contend for the region in a manner that we have traditionally not had to do. China's growing presence and long term commitment, amplified by President Xi Jinping's promise during the January 2015 China-CELAC meeting to promote investments valued at $250 billion over the next 10 years, is changing the economic and political dynamic. At the same time, Brazil's rise has been universally and appropriately praised, but with its interest in developing an increasing global profile, for example in the BRICS context, coupled with an increased capacity to realize greater ambitions, we must also recognize that Brazilian pursuit of its own foreign policy interests does not always coincide with our preferences. That's ok—competition is good in both politics and business. But it does mean that we have to engage meaningfully with the region on a sustained and creative basis, finding ways to promote our interests effectively by working closely in partnership with others wherever we can, while recognizing the rapidly changing nature of hemispheric relations.

In April, the next Summit of the Americas in Panama will be an important opportunity to lay out a concrete vision for regional engagement. Much work has already occurred, but the ground has shifted even from the previous Summit in Colombia and the competition to set and implement the regional agenda has increased. Promotion of strategic U.S. interests should guide our approach at the Summit in April and beyond. If it does, we can indeed look forward to the day when the hemisphere is middle class, fully democratic, and secure.

Thank you again Mr. Chairman and Mr. Ranking Minority Member for the opportunity to appear before you today. I look forward to your comments and questions.

Mr. DUNCAN. I want to thank all the witnesses for those great opening testimonies. You know, sitting here listening I am thinking we could talk about U.S. policy in Cuba, Venezuela and their energy sector and economic problems, unaccompanied children, upcoming elections in the region, Canada and Keystone Pipeline, Mexico reforms in the energy sector and other reforms or the 43 children and their death.

We could talk about Argentina and Alberto Nisman. We could talk about Iran and the Iranian threat and activity in the hemisphere, energy in the region, the opportunities in the Caribbean and energy as a whole, TPP and trade, trade and the Panama Canal, the successes in Colombia, and those were just the things I wrote down in the last 30 seconds of your statement.

There is a lot of different areas we could talk about and so let us get started. I recognize myself for 5 minutes and then I will take it to the ranking member and then in order.

One thing that concerns me and a lot of folks is the visa waiver program and what we see with terrorism acts in Paris and what the visa waiver program may mean going forward to safety and security in the United States.

And so, Ms. O'Neil, you talked about—a little bit about preclearance, which I think preclearance and visa waiver are two different issues but they are very similar.

One year ago this month, Chile was designated the 38th participant in the visa waiver program and Brazil and Uruguay have indicated an interest in that program, and so when I think about the Iranian threat in the Western Hemisphere, the visa waiver program and all of these things, I would like to ask you to delve into that a little bit more.

In a case such as these do you believe that it will take—what will it take for these countries—Uruguay and Brazil—to make necessary changes that you talked about in your statement in order to adapt the visa waiver program and what are your thoughts on that, just real quickly, and I am going to move on?

Ms. O'NEIL. Thank you. I mean, I think the preclearance type program—trusted traveller type programs of which visa waivers are part—can be a win-win situation and, one, because it allows us to process people faster but it also allows us to know who is coming and know a lot more about them than in traditional types of visa programs where you show up.

And so the electronic—you know, submitting electronic information, having the information well beyond that person travels anywhere near the U.S. borders actually can be quite useful.

Also, for countries to participate in these, as we have seen with Mexico and Canada which have much deeper and much broader types of programs because of the shared geographic borders, but in other countries that participate they too have a much better sense because of the types of standards they have to reach to participate with us.

They too have much more information about who is in their country, who is—you know, should be there, who should not, whether citizens or visitors or the like.

So I think in that sense in trying to make the whole region, the whole hemisphere more secure, in many ways visa waiver programs can be very helpful, because it encourages, if not forces, those countries to come up to some standards in terms of the information that they have about their own people residing in their country and those who might then apply to come and visit us.

Mr. DUNCAN. Right. Well, thank you for that and I will just for the record talk about Paraguay and a lot of the folks that come to Paraguay into that tri-border region on falsified documents and close proximity to Brazil and Uruguay really concerns me, and so thank you for that.

I just want to ask Dr. Ellis, did you read the Department of State's report on the Iranian threat in Western Hemisphere as required by Public Law 112–220?

Mr. ELLIS. I have read it.

Mr. DUNCAN. All five pages of it? So you talked a little bit about the Iranian threat. Do you think the State Department did the Public Law service in what they did?

I personally don't think they went far enough in what the law required and the intent. What are your thoughts on that?

Mr. ELLIS. Thank you very much. I think it is a wonderful question, sir. To me, the State Department was correct on a technicality, but missed some of the bigger issues. I think, certainly, under President Rouhani Iran has lowered its profile in the region.

It is unclear whether at the level—at the classified level whether things such as recruitment of radicals in Iran and Qom and other places and the madrassas continues or what the Quds Forces continue to do in the region.

But beyond what Iran is diplomatically doing previously under Ahmadinejad, what concerns me also is a continuing role through Iran and in others of organizations such as Hezbollah which, clearly, continue to finance activities often in combination with terrorist organizations, and even if Iran itself has lowered its profile, I think the activities of Islamic radicals continue to be a significant threat that we need to keep our eye on.

Mr. DUNCAN. Thank you. Something I will focus on is the Iranian threat. In the remaining time, I want talk to Ms. Glick about Colombia, the successes that we have seen in Colombia with the partnership, with the training there, helo pilots and the helicopter assistance the U.S. has given in pushing back the FARC and pushing back the narco trafficking.

How can we take that Colombia model, in your opinion, and apply it to maybe other countries in the region? Is there opportunity in Nicaragua and Honduras, in your experience there? How do you see that Colombia model maybe being transported to other areas?

Ms. GLICK. I think the key with Colombia is that we had an actively engaged partner in President Uribe in the time that we were negotiating and working with Plan Colombia. The United States invested, and I use that term deliberately, invested nearly $1 billion in Plan Colombia and we see a return on the investment.

President Uribe, President Santos—they are able to engage with law enforcement as well as coordinating across the military and with civil society as well. There is volume.

Mr. DUNCAN. You mentioned that. Let me ask you, do you think the judicial side of it—the civil society and judicial component of enforcement of rule of law—I personally think that is a vital aspect whether it is Mexico or whether it is Guatemala or whether it is other countries. So——

Ms. GLICK. That is entirely correct, sir, and to have that as a partner rather than just as an imposition from the United States, rather than us wagging our fingers and saying you have to do this, the Colombians actually did it and they took it on themselves to take back their country.

So if we can get that similar type of engagement in Central America with governments there, heck yeah, we can move forward and we can have successes like we have in Colombia.

Mr. DUNCAN. Are you familiar with what the Colombians are doing to train the law enforcement and judiciary folks from the Latin American countries, whether it is Guatemala, Honduras, Nicaragua? From what I understand, and I have seen some of it, some of the training, can you touch base on that?

Ms. GLICK. I think, sir, I will have to get back to you with a little bit more detail. But the region looks at Colombia as a success and it is wonderful to then be able to see the region taking care of the region and that is what Colombia is coming out as a leader and doing.

Mr. DUNCAN. I am going to highlight successes. Dr. O'Neil, are you familiar with what the Colombians are doing in that regard?

Ms. O'NEIL. I am familiar with that, and in particular some of the work that they have done in Mexico. General Naranjo came up and was an advisor to Pena Nieto who had been the head of the national police in Colombia before he just went back recently.

I think what is interesting when you think about models of Colombia for other places, particularly places like Mexico where all of us should have real concerns about, they have done the incredibly important economic reforms but they have yet to really institute a democratic rule of law and strengthen it throughout the country.

One of the big lessons from Colombia, to me, which you just touched on, is that they also—their society chimed in and participated with Uribe and so Uribe, along with the money that we provided and the help, also instituted a wealth tax and that money went just for security and to two things.

One, it gave them resources to fight the threats that they had, but it was also done in a very open and transparent way so there was not corruption involved.

That money didn't go in to the black hole of government, and so that also helped Colombia begin to clean up its institutions, which it has done. And so as Mexico or others, as we work with them, there are many things we can do, the Colombians can do as well.

But they also need to bring along their society and have people invest in their own country and the public good of democratic rule of law.

Mr. DUNCAN. All right. Well, thank you so much. My time is up. I will recognize the ranking member for 5 minutes.

Mr. SIRES. Thank you, Mr. Chairman.

Mr. Farnsworth, you know, as the price of oil declines it has taken a significant toll on other countries, especially in Venezuela. The Venezuelan people are suffering. Obviously, they have been suffering for a long time, shortages. Of course, President Maduro

59

now blames Vice President Biden for all the troubles that he is having.

Are we going to see mass protests? Are we—do you think he survives this? I mean, I have friends in Venezuela I talk to all the time and they can't even get sanitary paper.

Mr. FARNSWORTH. Well, thank you, sir, for the question. I think it is a critically important, one, not just for the Venezuelan people, but also for the region as a whole and the truth of the matter is nobody really knows.

That is certainly one thing that is being discussed actively at senior levels of councils all across the hemisphere. I would simply say that the situation has gotten dramatically worse, as you have said, since the death of Hugo Chavez.

President Maduro has for a number of reasons proven incapable to change the course of Venezuela economically. Certainly, the price of energy has contributed directly to that, but that is not the only reason why Venezuela is in trouble.

I would hesitate to sketch out what is going to happen and I think Yogi Berra had the great quote, "I don't want to make predictions about the future," but the fact of the matter is this is a very serious issue and it is an issue that I would contend isn't just for the United States.

I would like to see a very active role, for example, countries like Brazil, countries like Colombia, countries like Mexico, other regional countries to really take a leadership position here. At the recent meeting last week of the CELAC countries, for example, this did not seem to be a priority.

At the Summit of the Americas in April in Panama, it could be a priority, because ultimately if this goes from bad to worse or worse to worst, we are going to see a humanitarian crisis and I think that it is in nobody's interest, clearly, not the Venezuelan people.

Mr. SIRES. And I have read reports where supposedly Cuba has over 30,000 people in Venezuela and they are basically propping up the army and security.

I was just wondering, with all that and the declining of oil prices and all these Caribbean countries depending on Venezuela for petroleum, where do these countries go now if something happens there?

Mr. FARNSWORTH. Well, let me—if I can just follow up with that and then just a couple comments. But I think this was precisely the reason why the Vice President recently called together and then they met later with all, the leaders of the Caribbean Basin, to talk about energy security in the Caribbean Basin.

There are a number of things we can do on clean energy, for example, but one of the things I would like to see would be a much more aggressive use of natural gas exports into the Caribbean Basin.

It is a cleaner energy. It is plentiful in terms of the United States, and it is an energy source that could be employed in the Caribbean Basin with some improvements in terms of infrastructure, transportation, what have you.

But we have not, since the first Caribbean Basin initiative in the early 1980s, really seen the Caribbean Basin in a strategic way and

I think we have the opportunity now, certainly, because of the changes that have happened exogenously through the energy markets globally, we have the opportunity to change the way we look at the Caribbean Basin including Central America into a more strategic way with energy as an important tool that really undergirds that new approach.

Trade, energy, people to people, tourism, I mean, these are all issues that I think will go a very long way sort of to trying to address the question of where do these countries, which are in very difficult conditions financially, where do they go next and I think we can be an obvious answer to that.

Mr. SIRES. Dr. O'Neil?

Ms. O'NEIL. Let me just add one brief comment. One is that the cost of the end of subsidized oil is somewhat less, given the fallen oil prices.

So if these countries are buying on world markets it is much less than it would have been in the past. But I do think this is an area for North America, and as our production—Canada, United States and hopefully Mexico—with the changing rules, as our production of gas, of oil, of other energies increases that looking at the region, looking at stability and resiliency and particularly where the Caribbean fits in, I think this is an area where we can work with our neighbors to provide a much more secure local geography including them.

Mr. ELLIS. I just want to add two quick comments. One is that there are—not all of the nations in the Caribbean are particularly happy with the prospect of increased U.S. gas exports, specifically Trinidad and Tobago, and also while it does not always involve explicitly energy exports, China has stepped up in a major way offering credits to the region as we saw at the recent China CELAC conference in Beijing, and in many ways although energy dependence and worries about Venezuela plays favorably to the United States, as we saw from our recent initiative, it also helps to push those nations farther into the hands of China with respect to China's potential aid to them.

Mr. SIRES. You know, a few years ago—I go to Colombia often and a few years ago I had the opportunity to have dinner with one of the presidents of the university, and he made a statement to me.

He says that the second most foreign language studied in Colombia is Mandarin. Is that accurate? I assume it is. He told me but——

Mr. ELLIS. I suppose it depends on whether it is a public or private university. There definitely is a significant increase in Mandarin language studies.

A few years ago, to the extent that there was any knowledge in Colombia of Asia, it was primarily Japan. But we have certainly seen in some of the most prestigious universities, at Universidad Externado, Universidad de los Andes and others, there is an increase. But it is still a very marginal language.

Mr. SIRES. One last question. Of the report of 30,000 Cubans in Venezuela, do you think that is accurate?

Mr. ELLIS. It very well may be if you combine the doctors and medical trainers and others and, of course, the reports of significant penetration of the Venezuelan intelligence services.

Mr. SIRES. Thank you. Thank you, Mr. Chairman.

Mr. DUNCAN. Ms. Ros-Lehtinen from Florida, 5 minutes.

Ms. ROS-LEHTINEN. I don't want to jump ahead of anybody here because I came kind of last.

Mr. DUNCAN. Actually, you are next on the list.

Ms. ROS-LEHTINEN. All right. I like it.

Mr. DUNCAN. I believe so.

Ms. ROS-LEHTINEN. Well, then thank you so much. Mr. Chairman, as we look around the region, as these wonderful panelists have pointed out, what we see is deeply troubling.

Democracy has been slowly eroding in the countries in the region by the hands of elected tyrants who use populist promises of reform and change and then they twist their systems into convenient arrangements where they retain the final word.

And one needs no further proof to see how countries are following this undemocratic principles and have changed their constitutions to fit their whims like Venezuela, Bolivia, Ecuador, Nicaragua, and leaders of these countries do not believe in the rule of law, separation of powers, constitutional order, free and fair elections, an impartial judicial system.

We have seen how these leftist experiments have led many countries to curtail basic freedoms. These illegitimate institutions are often utilized for the financial advantage of members of their own regime to illicitly make money off the backs of their own suffering people.

And corruption is one of the greatest problems facing the region at this point. An economy tainted with corruption cannot sustain an environment necessary to create the conditions for greater economic development.

Venezuela is a good example of this. It is a sham of a country, and it is in great deal of corruption going on there. You see the store shelves literally empty yet Maduro goes on all of these fancy trips.

They have archaic systems like artificial currency controls that are exploited by the connected elites and denied to the private sector.

Many surrounding the regime have made themselves rich at the expense of the average Venezuelan, giving rise to the phenomenon of a self-professing socialist who display a great preference for owning luxury homes and luxury vehicles.

And just recently Maduro arrested Venezuelans for the gall of having them wait in line for food, and has gone so far as arresting pharmaceutical executives and blaming them for the medical shortages in the country.

In reality, as we know, Maduro has no one to blame but himself, and these are corrupt practices that are reprehensible and cannot but hurt the welfare of the people. Without a doubt, they are contributing factors to the near state of collapse that we see in Venezuela's economy.

And against corrupt abuses of this sort the U.S. must always be vigilant and its goal—our goal should always be clear to support and defend those who fight to expose and fight to end corruption.

So I ask the panelists how can the United States help tackle institutional corruption in our own hemisphere. Is it possible to use the economic influence of our great country in the hemisphere in order to channel those countries into real and substantive democratic reforms?

And is organized crime and a plummeting economy directed by Venezuela a security risk for the entire hemisphere, specifically for Caribbean countries? And I will leave it to anyone who would like to testify. Dr. Ellis, I think you were going to testify.

Mr. ELLIS. Thank you—a wonderful question. For me, actually corruption is one of the centers of gravity for attacking the real malaise that is going on across the Americas right now.

If I could quickly make another observation—that as was rightfully pointed out, Venezuela not only is a tragedy for some people, it is also a tragedy for the rest of the region.

We can talk, for example, about Leamsy Salazar who recently came as cooperating with U.S. authorities and has made the claim that the current head of the Venezuelan Parliament, Diosdado Cabello, is actually the head of the largest narco trafficking organization, Cartel de los Soles.

Essentially, the record amounts of cocaine that we are seeing coming through the Caribbean as well as destabilization of the Columbian borderlands, other places like that, Venezuela is not simply a problem for its own people.

But with respect to corruption itself, there are in part technical solutions that our own engagement through State and DoD can support. There are some interesting things with respect to both institutionalization of things like lie detector tests but also institutional support.

You had a case in Honduras not too long ago where a significant portion of the police force was identified as being corrupted and none of them were fired. So I think it is a combination of diplomatic pressure and others.

But also I think a holistic whole of government solution is critical, because corruption is important to reestablishing the connection between the citizens and the government. Alvaro Uribe was mentioned before and to me part of the magic of what the success of Colombia is, and our Mexican allies hate when we gringos talk to them about the lessons of Colombia.

But to me part of what was the systematic concept, the idea that you have to reestablish the faith of the government in its people and with that you get intelligence and investment and everything else.

And so as I look at some of our plans, one of the things that I think is very important is that we not just add together individual programs but that we think about how are we going, little by little, to fight this systematically. Thank you.

Ms. ROS-LEHTINEN. Thank you so much and I regret that I am out of time. Thank you , Mr. Chairman. Thank you, Dr. Ellis.

Mr. DUNCAN. Thank you, and, you know, with the Summit of the Americas coming up it is important to think about these issues and hopefully we can lead a congressional delegation there.

The next gentleman that I am going to recognize has spent a lot of time in Latin America developing relationships. I saw that first hand on a Codel Royce back in November. So, Mr. Meeks, you are recognized for 5 minutes.

Mr. MEEKS. Thank you, Mr. Chairman, and, you know, we looked at the challenges and I guess the—there is a lot of progress in the region also and you have nations like Brazil and Chile and Colombia and Uruguay and they are not just keeping economic gains at home.

In fact, what I think is significant that they are sharing them in the form of now they are giving foreign aid themselves to some other countries, and democracies like Peru and Panama that have stood the test of time on making tremerdous progress against unrelenting inequality, and they are growing the middle class and poverty is starting to reduce in those areas.

And just a few days ago, Prime Minister Portia Simpson-Miller of Jamaica spoke here at the House about the enduring advancement in her nation and I am sure that there are many other CARICOM nations that are moving forward there.

And then, you know, but I want to ask another quick question. I think that, Mr. Farnsworth, looking at the Council of the Americas, I don't know, you all had something—you were either talking to somebody I need to talk to but when I looked at your latest issue where you talk about Cuba and Colombia or political change and peace finally at hand you must have known something that we didn't know.

This was in advance of some of the announcements that have come out and you talk about in there also though, which I want to ask a quick question about, which has been something that I have worked on a lot in Colombia and that is the plight of African Colombians because they are still in the middle as, you know, with negotiating peace they are still in the middle of the FARC battle and violence is happening in that area, et cetera.

So given what is going on all over the place, could you basically just give us a quick—and there is a good article in this issue, by the way, on the plight of African Colombians in the middle of this war zone still continuing?

Mr. FARNSWORTH. Well, Mr. Meeks thanks for the opportunity and thank you for the plug for our magazine. We appreciate it very much.

You are really truly the expert on these issues so I hesitate to try even to respond to your question, but simply to say that these are not only critically important issues but they are issues that need to be addressed seriously because they stem from history, they stem from culture but they also stem from the idea of economic exclusion and when you—when you have societies that don't fully value every person in society be it Afro-Colombians, be in the indigenous population, being folks with physical disabilities, what have you, this is critically important for the long-term development of the region as a prosperous middle class region that I think we all seek.

You cannot pursue the same type of economic model across the region that has traditionally been pursued, which is to say that a certain smaller number of elites have access to power, have access to the levers of the economy, have access to the judicial system and can advance themselves and their families whereas the broader majority of people don't have the same access.

And that is what we have seen in some way as driving these changes that we have seen across the Western Hemisphere over the last 10 years or so, which is to say as democracy itself has become much more institutionalized, and that is a very good thing. You now have traditionally marginalized populations, which have access to political power and have been voting into power people, who want to make sure that the benefits of the modern state accrue to the broader population.

That is a very good thing, in my judgment. Having said that, that does bring political changes and sometimes there are leaders who take a mandate and go too far with it, as we have seen from some of the countries that have already been mentioned.

In the case of Colombia, however, I think it is accurate to say that the Colombian Government is aware of the issue, recognizes that more needs to be done, recognizes fundamentally that peace has to come to the region for all of Colombia, but also that you can't just then bring peace and say okay, our job is done—that you then have to proactively work with the affected communities in terms of economic development, in terms of social inclusion and all the things that we might take for granted here in the United States.

Mr. MEEKS. Thank you, Mr. Farnsworth. Let me ask Dr. O'Neil a quick question because I agree with you. I am a big supporter of TPP and I think that it will go a long way.

I believe that the groups that I am looking for like African Colombian and others benefit. In fact, when you look at Peru as they reduce their poverty some of it is because of the economic growth that they were able to gain as a result of our trade agreement with them.

But, now, as we move toward TPP we know that—my question to you would be is how would TPP affect the U.S. trade relationships with other—with our existing partners like Colombia?

Is it—will it also open the opportunity to more negotiation, maybe going back to talk about trade with the Americas—that when I first arrived at Congress we were talking about trade with the Americas, all of the, you know, countries in Latin America and in South America?

Ms. O'NEIL. Well, many of our partners within the Western Hemisphere are included in the TPP negotiations. Colombia is not yet, as you well know, but would very much like to be included.

So I think setting up this platform there is then an opening for countries like Colombia who would want to come in and accept what is—what has been negotiated and join this and one of the real benefits is as we look at world trade over the last 30 years it has changed in the way it is done in almost every country.

We are not sending finished goods. We are sending—the majority of things are pieces and parts that are moving back and forth. And so in that free trade agreements are increasingly important in the Western Hemisphere, because it allows this comparative advantage that many countries have. It allows us to work together to create competitive products that can be sent wherever they are around the world.

So I think these types of agreements, TPP, are incredibly important for actually bringing benefits and particularly the value added side that Ms. Glick was talking about. That is the future for us in the United States but also for these countries, for these middle classes for what we hope for them and we hope to work together with. And so there I do agree with you.

I think these trade agreements are vital that we do that, and that once it is decided between the current negotiating partners that we open it up to those that want to join and some will not want to join, as we well know, but others will and so there is an open platform for them to join with us in this increasingly regional but global agreement.

Mr. MEEKS. Thank you.

Mr. DUNCAN. Thank you. The gentleman's time has expired and now the Chair will recognize the newest member of the committee on the Republican side, Mr. Emmer, from Minnesota, for 5 minutes.

Mr. EMMER. New Minnesota. Thank you, Mr. Chair, and Dr. O'Neil, if I could take you back. In your written testimony you advocate for energy to "become a fundamental pillar of North America's new partnership."

If you could give a little bit more detail how should Canada, Mexico, and the U.S. work to deepen our trilateral relationship on energy and if you wouldn't mind since in reference to an earlier question—I don't remember who asked it but we were talking about the Caribbean Basin, maybe expand it into that.

Ms. O'NEIL. I think there are many ways that we could deepen our ties, and right now is a very important moment to do so in part because Mexico is changing the rules in its energy sector.

After 70-plus years of being closed and having been controlled only by a state-owned enterprise it is now going to be open for private investment and in the coming months they are going to do their first auctions, allowing in all sorts of national or all international energy companies, and it is really a time to right the rules there to create a very open, transparent, competitive and safe industry that will affect us, given our geographic proximity.

So it is a moment to do so. I mean, one of the biggest things I believe is infrastructure, and we have seen with both of our neighbors, these are two of our largest energy partners and trade goes back and forth each way and if we deepen that these are also areas—these are democracies.

These are open societies. Of course, there are some issues here and there but these are very stable, you know, energy partners compared to many other places around the world which we have talked about even here in the Western Hemisphere.

But if we can tie ourselves we actually provide a very stable, but also resilience is very important for our energy sector. I live in New York City and back a couple years ago when Hurricane Sandy came in we understood for 2 weeks what it is like not to have power, what it is like to be without energy and the importance of resilience in our system whether it is electricity, whether it is gas supplies and the others is vital for economic production but just for our well-being.

In fact, in that particular moment our ties with Canada both in terms of our electricity grids but our agreements with utility companies brought New York City and the area much more quickly, and I do believe, now that Mexico is changing, we can do the same thing along the southern border and to benefit all the states that are along that border and even those further in, providing a resiliency there so that if there are problems in the power grid, whether it is because of overloading or whether it is because of cyber security and other challenges that we will have as we go forward, infrastructure is vitally important to make sure these flows are safe back and forth.

And the other thing, let me just mention quickly, is this side of we are a geographic region together and we have one of the biggest economic blocs, and so what we decide to do on energy and the mix we have in terms of clean and renewable and other types of traditional will affect the world.

And so as we think about how we will change it over the next several years and decades, doing it with our neighbors is increasingly vital. So as we set energy guidelines, standards for cars, for safety and the like that, too, will be important to make sure that the economic benefits stay within the region so that we don't have differing types of regulations between Canada, between the United States and Mexico.

So when you are a company, a manufacturer or others you think about the region, the types of systems you had put in place or the types of energy choices you make you will be doing it within a region and particularly given, as I was speaking about, this underlying economic production platform that happens now that is occurring in North America, having energy incentives align across the three countries I think is very important as we grow on that economic side.

Mr. EMMER. You know, if you could expand on that just a little bit, because the security issues in Mexico are a little bit different than the security issues we face in Canada, and you talk about infrastructure and I would agree completely.

But how do you ensure or what can we do to ensure that it can be done first so that you attract private investment because they want to realize a return but that you can do it in a low risk safe manner, cost effective manner?

Is there anything the U.S. should be considering in that regard as you move forward with, for instance, Mexico?

Ms. O'NEIL. In the energy sector in particular in that narrow area there are things we can do and many, you know, international oil companies are used to dealing in areas that are quite risky.

And so they have some means of doing it already, systems in place for some types of things. But overall, I think this gets to our larger relationship with Mexico and I believe right now Mexico is at really a fundamental place.

It has done, I would want to acknowledge, an incredible set of economic reforms that can set that country up for growth and prosperity down the road.

But it has yet to really grapple with the corruption in rule of law and we are seeing that over just the last few months some of the challenges.

But in every crisis there is an opportunity and so if his government decides that for their legacy and for Mexico for the future to really take on corruption, to change the rules that are there, to try to dive in and create a new justice system, which is already happening but which has been slow to be implemented, if they do take this on and make it their priority I think we can come in whether through the Merida Initiative or other types of programs that we have and help them do that, and they will need to do things like retrain almost 40,000 lawyers and judges and official clerks in the new justice system and we have lawyers and other organizations that can do that.

We can help bring in Colombians or others, as we were speaking about, who know how to professionalize police forces. There are things we can do to help this government when they decide to step in.

Mr. EMMER. Thank you very much. I see my time has expired.

Mr. DUNCAN. Thank you. Great line of questioning. When we were there on Codel Royce in November in Mexico a lot of the things you talk about, Dr. O'Neil, were discussed, and just for the record we were there when the 43 children were still missing before they found any remains and demonstrations in Mexico City of basically college-age kids and the paintings of the children and themselves that were missing it was quite moving.

But one thing we did we met with civil society about the corruption and bribery that goes on within the judicial system of folks that are arrested so having someone there as a public advocate and what they are trying to do.

I think the reforms if they—if they take hold I think it absolutely right that Mexico will benefit from that economically, and so I am excited about some of the things you talked about.

Great line of questions, especially on the energy sector. Cross border energy, whether it is our natural gas and Mexico's development of their natural gas but the electrical grid is already shared in certain border towns and so how do we work with our members.

So thanks for that line of questioning, Tom, and I will now yield 5 minutes to the gentleman from California, Mr. Lowenthal.

Mr. LOWENTHAL. Well, thank you. First of all, my goals have been met. I really came just to learn and to listen. I have learned a lot about corruption.

I have learned more about energy, trade, security issues, economic development, drugs. But I am going to ask a question or two. I want to switch to something that Mr. Farnsworth said about talking about how these—how nations are in our hemisphere are beginning to deal with some of the marginalized populations.

Just recently, Senator Markey—I don't think you know—Senator Markey and I introduced legislation that would direct the Department of State to further demonstrate its commitment to the LGBT human rights as a foreign policy priority of the United States by establishing a position within the State Department in the Bureau of Democracy, Human Rights and Labor just for to deal with LGBT issues.

I wondered if you could talk to me a little bit about either Mr. Farnsworth or anybody else on the panel really the state of affairs with regard to the LGBT community in the Western Hemisphere.

We know that there are some nations like Jamaica, Honduras where the plight—where I am very concerned and many of us are very concerned about the plight of the LGBT community.

Yet there are other countries like Uruguay and Costa Rica where there have been tremendous positive movement. And I am wondering how do we begin to deal with it in terms of U.S. interests as we begin to really begin to focus on human rights issues whether it is Cuba or anywhere in the states. Is this an issue that we can play some role in?

Mr. FARNSWORTH. Well, thank you very much for the question and welcome to the subcommittee.

Mr. LOWENTHAL. Thank you.

Mr. FARNSWORTH. It is very nice to see you again, Mr. Lowenthal. You know, these are issues that fit squarely within the concept of social inclusion and, again, the idea that everybody has a unique and important role to play in the development of the country based on their unique characteristics and you cannot by law or legislation or informally exclude whole sectors of society.

That just doesn't work anymore. And so you ask what are some of the things the United States can do. Well, in the first instance, education I think is critically important.

The idea that some behaviors simply are not acceptable, and I think this is something that the State Department has tried to do and is doing a little bit more of, can do more—other governments as well.

But like anything these are some difficult issues. They are long ingrained within the Western Hemisphere. Each country is different. Each community within countries can be different at times and I think the real answer is just to keep pushing, keep raising consciousness, if we can use that term of art that was popular some time ago, but the idea that certain behaviors are just not acceptable in a region that values democracy, that values human rights and that values the individual uniqueness of every of its citizens.

Mr. LOWENTHAL. Anybody else want to take a stab at that?

Ms. GLICK. Quick stab at it. You mentioned Uruguay which was, I think, the first country in the world that legalized gay marriage.

Mr. LOWENTHAL. Yes.

Ms. GLICK. It is one of these things that this is the arc of history that you are seeing move right before our eyes quickly in the United States as well as in other countries in the world. As Mr. Farnsworth said, these are long ingrained traditions.

There is a lot of impact that comes from various religious groups as well. I think that it is—the easiest way to look at this is the same way in which we look at issues related to the LGBT community in the Unites States. They are going to have an impact.

There will be changes in some countries. There won't be changes in others in the long or in the short term, and it will be an interesting thing to watch and see progress.

But I think in terms of social inclusion and engaging with civil society this too is something that is going to come largely from the populations themselves, and is it really one of the things that the United States has to raise the flag about.

I am not entirely sure that it is our responsibility or even our right to do so. We can call out human rights violations and hate crimes when we see them. I think that is very valuable.

But I think in terms of these populations and communities in their own countries they can look to the United States for examples and they can look to other countries in the region as well as examples.

Mr. LOWENTHAL. Thank you. I too want to keep raising the issues like marginalized populations on this committee. I want to maybe just quickly, if I have a minute, I have heard a lot about the development of the energy sector, the interdependence between and the relationship between the United States and our partners.

I haven't heard very much about except a little bit from Dr. O'Neil about renewable energy, climate change, a real—is there—what kind of commitment? Would anybody really like to address that? Dr. Ellis.

Mr. ELLIS. Thank you very much. There actually is considerable progress in renewable energy across the Americas. I actually can say this is one of the areas in which China, for better or worse, has been beneficial with respect to the combination of low cost loans and other things.

When we look at countries such as Ecuador, but other countries such as Brazil, we find tremendous advances in the hydroelectric sector although that, of course, has side impacts on things such as local populations who live there and that has created problems as well.

Significant impacts in solar—the number one Chinese investment, over $1 billion, programmed in Chile is not in copper but is actually in the north of the country in solar power.

And so in many ways we do see that leadership, I think, in renewable in part through the United States but in part through other actors as well, and Japan and others have played constructive roles in that as well.

Mr. LOWENTHAL. Thank you.

Mr. DUNCAN. The gentleman's time has expired. I am going to allow just briefly if you would like to chime in—I know Mr. Farnsworth wanted to just real briefly.

Mr. FARNSWORTH. Thanks, sir. Just one statistic—Latin America has the cleanest energy matrix of any region in the world based on hydro, based on some of the renewable in their energy matrix, and therefore, is an obvious partner for us in developing some of these issues.

Mr. DUNCAN. Yes. Thank you. Only because I like you. No, I am just kidding.

Well, that concludes—in the sense of time that concludes the hearing. I think the panelists have been absolutely fabulous, very insightful in providing information, today, I think that we have all benefitted from. I am going to ask that the record will remain open for 10 days for submission of remarks or extraneous materials that might be beneficial to the overall concept of the hearing.

I look forward to having further conversations with all the panelists as we go forward. I plan on helping America focus on this hemisphere and rebuilding some ties and relationships which I think are very, very important.

I look forward to working with the ranking member, and I appreciate his input and with that the committee will stand adjourned.

[Whereupon, at 12:41 p.m., the subcommittee was adjourned.]

APPENDIX

MATERIAL SUBMITTED FOR THE RECORD

SUBCOMMITTEE HEARING NOTICE
COMMITTEE ON FOREIGN AFFAIRS
U.S. HOUSE OF REPRESENTATIVES
WASHINGTON, DC 20515-6128

Subcommittee on the Western Hemisphere
Jeff Duncan (R-SC), Chairman

TO: MEMBERS OF THE COMMITTEE ON FOREIGN AFFAIRS

You are respectfully requested to attend an OPEN hearing of the Committee on Foreign Affairs, to be held by the Subcommittee on the Western Hemisphere in Room 2172 of the Rayburn House Office Building (and available live on the Committee website at http://www.ForeignAffairs.house.gov):

DATE: Tuesday, February 3, 2015

TIME: 11:00 a.m.

SUBJECT: The Strategic Importance of the Western Hemisphere: Defining U.S. Interests in the Region

WITNESSES: Shannon K. O'Neil, Ph.D.
Senior Fellow for Latin America Studies
Council on Foreign Relations

Ms. Bonnie Glick
Senior Vice President
GlobalConnect Division
Meridian International Center

Evan Ellis, Ph.D.
Author

Mr. Eric Farnsworth
Vice President
Council of the Americas and Americas Society

By Direction of the Chairman

COMMITTEE ON FOREIGN AFFAIRS

MINUTES OF SUBCOMMITTEE ON _____ *Western Hemisphere* _____ HEARING

Day___ *Tuesday* ___Date___ *February 3, 2015* ___Room_____ *2172*_____

Starting Time ___*11:00 a.m.*___ Ending Time ___*12:41 p.m.*___

Recesses _____ (____to ____) (____to ____) (____to ____) (____to ____) (____to ____) (____to ____)

Presiding Member(s)

Chairman Jeff Duncan

Check all of the following that apply:

Open Session ☑   Electronically Recorded (taped) ☑
Executive (closed) Session ☐   Stenographic Record ☑
Televised ☑

TITLE OF HEARING:

"The Strategic Importance of the Western Hemisphere: Defining the U.S. Interests in the Region"

SUBCOMMITTEE MEMBERS PRESENT:

Reps. Duncan, Ros-Lehtinen, Salmon, DeSantis, Yoho, Emmer, Sires, Castro, Kelly, Meeks, Lowenthal

NON-SUBCOMMITTEE MEMBERS PRESENT: *(Mark with an * if they are not members of full committee.)*

HEARING WITNESSES: Same as meeting notice attached? Yes ☑ No ☐
(If "no", please list below and include title, agency, department, or organization.)

STATEMENTS FOR THE RECORD: *(List any statements submitted for the record.)*

TIME SCHEDULED TO RECONVENE _____
or
TIME ADJOURNED ___*12:41 p.m.*___

Subcommittee Staff Director

WRITTEN RESPONSES FROM MR. ERIC FARNSWORTH, VICE PRESIDENT, COUNCIL OF THE AMERICAS AND AMERICAS SOCIETY, TO QUESTIONS SUBMITTED FOR THE RECORD BY THE HONORABLE JEFF DUNCAN, A REPRESENTATIVE IN CONGRESS FROM THE STATE OF SOUTH CAROLINA, AND CHAIRMAN, SUBCOMMITTEE ON THE WESTERN HEMISPHERE

"The Strategic Importance of the Western Hemisphere:
Defining U.S. Interests in the Region"

Hearing by the Western Hemisphere Subcommittee of the
House Foreign Affairs Committee
February 3, 2015

Questions for the Record

Eric Farnsworth
Vice President, Council of the Americas

Question

"U.S. assistance to the region has fallen in each of the past four fiscal years, declining $1.9 billion in FY 2011 to $1.5 billion in FY 2014. What effects have cuts in assistance had on U.S. bilateral relations and influence in Latin America and the Caribbean? To what extent do you think the foreign assistance budget for the region should be reoriented toward different priorities? Aside from foreign aid, what other forms of engagement might the U.S. government use to advance its policy priorities in the region?"

Answer

I have long argued that foreign assistance to the countries of the Western Hemisphere should be increased not decreased, because a marginal increase in assistance there has a greater positive impact on U.S. policy goals than equivalent aid increases elsewhere. Nonetheless, it seems, U.S. assistance to Latin America and the Caribbean is generally the first region to suffer under declining foreign aid scenarios. This gives the impression that the United States is relatively disinterested in engaging with the region over the longer term, and opens doors wider to those who do not necessarily share our values, including Venezuela and outside actors including China, to fill a perceived void.

Certainly, U.S. foreign assistance must be targeted and well-considered in order to be effective. We should increase assistance to build on successes, while cutting back where assistance has proven less effective. For example, much previous support has gone to Colombia, and the United States will again be called on to support implementation of peace accords once they are agreed. This is manifestly in our national interests, and should be actively considered as a follow on to successful support for the original Plan Colombia, a noteworthy bipartisan foreign policy success.

In terms of foreign aid delivery, the Millennium Challenge Corporation (MCC) continues to be an appropriate, additive model. To increase the effectiveness of such assistance, income thresholds must be changed in order to increase the number of eligible countries. The program should also be amended so that MCC compacts can be concluded with sub-regions under a certain income threshold, such as Southern Mexico and Northeastern Brazil, apart from national compacts, thus increasing eligibilities.

Substantively, I would like to see a much greater emphasis for U.S. assistance on investment climate reforms, trade facilitation including customs procedures, infrastructure, and democracy and good governance. Building economic efficiencies and sound growth strategies will, over time, do much more to build sustainable economic growth in the region. This supports U.S. economic priorities while also creating conditions ultimately reducing the need for direct economic support in the first place.

At the same time, the region arguably faces a greater threat to democratic governance today than at any time since the first Summit of the Americas in 1994. Support for democratic ideals and practices must therefore remain a core aspect of U.S. foreign assistance to the region: strong and independent governing institutions; transparent, regular, and legitimately contested elections; freedom of the press and freedom of speech and assembly; a robust human rights agenda; and the full slate of guarantees listed within the Inter-American Democratic Charter.

The United States also maintains significant additional tools beyond direct assistance. The power of markets and the desire for investments continues to capture the imagination of much of the region, while economic indicators such as interest rates, currency values, and actions of the Federal Reserve have profound implications. Even countries that purposefully pursue unproductive diplomatic relations with the United States including Bolivia, Ecuador, Nicaragua, Venezuela, and others, seek to maintain access to the U.S. market while looking to attract additional investments from North America. As a consequence, the United States should take a more active approach to trade and investment expansion in the Western Hemisphere, working in the first instance with those countries that want to build closer economic relations with us. Examples of steps to consider include the prompt conclusion and passage of the Trans-Pacific Partnership (TPP) which includes Canada, Mexico, Peru, and Chile; the rapid incorporation of Colombia and perhaps certain nations in Central America into a completed TPP and also APEC; incorporation of both Canada and Mexico into the Trans-Atlantic Trade and investment Partnership negotiations with Europe; active support for the Pacific Alliance which currently includes four of our regional free trade partners; consolidation of existing hemispheric trade agreements under one omnibus umbrella to the TPP or other high standard level; and heightened efforts to engage Brazil and other MERCOSUR nations such as Paraguay and Uruguay toward expanded, freer trade.

Given a fundamental shift in global energy markets, the United States should also find ways to develop a more active and effective energy diplomacy strategy for the region, centered on the export of cleaner, plentiful natural gas, particularly to the Caribbean Basin. Agriculture cooperation would be a meaningful area for true partnership. Security assistance, including assistance to combat growing cybercrime, must continue to be employed. Finally, the United States should prioritize the Western Hemisphere within international financial institutions including the IMF and World Bank, while working diligently as a priority of hemispheric policy to engage meaningfully and continuously with regional organizations of which we are a member, including the IDB, OAS, PAHO, and ECLAC.

"The Strategic Importance of the Western Hemisphere:
Defining U.S. Interests in the Region"

Hearing by the Western Hemisphere Subcommittee of the
House Foreign Affairs Committee
February 3, 2015

Questions for the Record

Eric Farnsworth
Vice President, Council of the Americas

Question

"Central American countries are struggling to deal with high levels of crime and
violence. The U.S. government has sought to assist the region through the Central
America Regional Security Initiative (CARSI), for which Congress has appropriated
about $1.1 billion since FY2008. To what extent do high levels of crime and violence in
Central America pose a threat to U.S. interests? In your judgment, how effective is
CARSI in addressing the challenges of crime and violence in the region? What
additional measures can the U.S. government take to address the situation in Central
America?"

Answer

High levels of crime and violence in Central America pose a fundamental threat to U.S.
interests in the region because they reduce economic growth by discouraging
investment—both domestic and foreign—while causing significant expenditures on non-
productive activities. Of course, the illegal drugs trade also injures the United States by
bringing illicit and harmful products into the country while requiring significant security
and healthcare expenditures in response. At the same time, criminal activities including
corruption have a corrosive effect on governance and, ultimately, democracy, by
hollowing out government institutions and reducing public trust. As a consequence, U.S.
prestige is impacted, because the brutal wars of the 1980's were fought in part to develop
democracy in the region. Anything that subsequently debilitates Central American
democracy is a set-back.

CARSI is a well-intentioned effort which has had success. As last summer's crisis of
unaccompanied migrant children from Central America reminds us, however, much more
must be done. For example, the Administration is requesting some $1 billion in
additional support for its "Plan for the Alliance for Prosperity in the Northern Triangle of
Central America," which ought to be considered actively by Congress. Nonetheless, the
key aspect of any successful regional strategy must be that Central America itself lead the
effort, including mobilization of resources, while taking concrete, meaningful steps to
create a true *regional* strategy. In short, Central American nations must work better
together, as a group, and U.S. assistance should encourage such actions.

For example, there should be one strategy for attracting investment, with consistent regional regulations rather than strictly national regulations. There should be one strategy for security, with regional implementation rather than national implementation. There should be one resource mobilization effort, rather than strictly national efforts, with the proceeds going to regional actions with full transparency and accountability. U.S. assistance can support this effort by appropriating and spending assistance to encourage regional versus national efforts, including regional police training, regional command and control, regional criminal labs, regional energy grids, regional infrastructure and customs modernization efforts, and regional administration of justice, just to name a few.

Central America is not Colombia; Plan Colombia has been quite successful and offers numerous lessons but it is not necessarily a template for Central America. In large measure, this is due to the fact that Colombia is one nation with one government and one economy with the uniform goal of fighting organized guerrilla groups. Central America is much more diffuse, with a metastasized threat, separate legal authorities and systems of governance, different histories in terms of political ideologies, human rights and the use of security forces to address both internal and external threats, and economic structures. To be most effective, additional U.S. assistance to Central America should be conditioned upon both the prospect and the reality of regional leaders pulling in the same direction, with the same intensity and commitment to common goals.